Light
That Bends
When It Passes

by Phoebe Frank

Edited by Rhoda Blecker

Cover by Tony Radford:
Granny Stone Design & Print

Illustrations by Phoebe Frank

Permanent Press
Calabasas, California, USA
1996

Library of Congress Cataloging-in-Publication Data

Phoebe Frank

   Light That Bends When It Passes

   1. short stories   2. personal poetry

ISBN 0-914615-24-6

Library of Congress Catalog Card Number: 95-073269

Manufactured in the United States of America

Permanent Press Publishing Co.
4363 Park Milano
Calabasas, CA 91302
(818) 222-8599

In conjunction with:
Isaac Nathan Publishing Co., Inc.
Woodland Hills, CA 91364
(818) 225-9631

Contents

In appreciation to my husband, Werner, who made this book possible.

Special thanks to my daughter Dori Kremer and good friend Charney Herst who served as readers, and who were undaunted by my peculiar spelling and idiosyncratic grammer.

To the character in the book who visited me in off hours, weekends and midnight, and who, upon publication, threw themselves a cast party and complained that none of their roles were big enough.

Light That Bends When It Passes

DELIA, MY DAUGHTER, KNEW SHE LOOKED GOOD IN HATS, even when other people weren't wearing them, even if the season was wrong. She liked to drape scarves around them, and ribbons and cloth cabbage roses. She could get away with straw in the winter and velvet in summer, she didn't depend on the weather to tell her what to do.

She wore a hat out in back of her house by the lake, black hair against a large white brimmed Panama that shaded her face. "Freckles," she said. "Don't need them, don't want them." A heart-shaped face topped with luxuriant hair which she wore in a braid. It rode down her back like a thick black rope that helped her not evaporate into the sky, like a plumb line that kept her tied to the earth .

I remembered how Delia filled up her white straw hat with wild strawberries that we and the grandchildren picked around the lake. The fruit stained the crown, but that was no problem. She just spread her acrylic paints out on the summer porch table and painted the blotches into a new design.

In summer, Delia's art studio was out on the screened-in porch. It had a northern exposure with a view of the lake and olive and pepper trees, planted by the former owner. She was given to painting large abstract canvasses that she brought down to the small beach where she dipped them in the water. Then she took paint by the buckets and sloshed it about until it made lovely ripple effects. After the paintings dried in the sun, she took the same canvass and repeated the technique, building up layers of watery colors. I've never been one for abstract art, but apparently they were quite good since she was represented by a respected Los Angeles gallery. What I liked best were her animal studies.

She had a gift for delineating a horse's leg just so. Horses have their legs put on all wrong. Their back ones bend funny and their front ones aren't much better. Delia liked to draw horses and lions, elephants even, and these designs she sold for lady's fashions, scarves and blouses.

I thought about that when I got to the hospital, standing just outside her room, not wanting to go in, not wanting to see her, more worried about how I would handle it than how she would. I had wanted her to walk the high wire, to balance herself out there in the world with a little pink parasol, as I never had. And now she lay white as aspirin under white sheets.

I didn't want to look at her. I would rather think about that big house on the lake, long gone now. I loved the way the lawn smelled at twilight after a lingering hot day. Roots shriveled, giving up their last bit of moisture just before sunset. The grass was ready to die and suddenly the night curved down like a knife slicing the sun into thin, translucent orange sections. Then the shoots of grass licked a little moisture out of the air and revived.

Lake Aston was a small disk of water that shimmered summer heat as though the sun had fallen between the parched hills and splattered into unmanageable puddles. There was the scent of something sifted and sweet in the air; ripening pears and broken geranium stems, pine needles and the scent of that tentative mold that grows on cheese. The deep green mesh of shadows surrounded us, nets that caught the summer and made it wriggle.

The children splashed in the water at dusk, but if I looked at them too hard, they seemed to disappear into the gloaming. Too soon they gave up being babies at the edge of the shore and jumped into row boats to paddle across the lake. Delia and I yelling, "Don't go too far, come back before dark."

I knew they'd come back early enough because my grand daughter Ronnie, who was then six, was with them. She was afraid to swim in my pool, as well as the lake, because she was afraid of sharks. She had to pull me into the living room, far away from everyone else to tell me her secret fear.

"Sharks," I said. "No, there aren't sharks. Dolphins, maybe. Mermaids even, but no sharks." I hugged her and the banished sharks were seen only occasionally after that.

Delia's husband, Arthur, did not usually get back to the house by the lake before dark. He worked in Century City, some kind of stock broker. Doing quite well, selling long when he should, and converting shorts at the right time.

He was a perfectly nice fellow but a bit tense about the eyes, as though he had just remembered something he should have done, but didn't.

The kids swam in my pool and in Delia and Arthur's lake. She and Arthur were happy then. She had just redone the big house all by herself. All the windows were tucked with Roman shades that disappeared into the ceiling allowing the sunshine to stream in as though it was a searchlight hunting for flaws. She favored earth tones; brown like burnt toast scraped light, petrified wood that died from old age turning in on it, translucent capsules of cod liver oil, the brown pink of her dog's tongue, the hypnotic smell of shoe polish that leads to leather dreams.

No heavy English curtains or chintz for her. "None of those bird cage cover fabrics for me, Mom. And no bird cage," she said as she unwrapped the house warming gift we gave them a month after they moved in — a decorative Victorian bird cage. Then she added hastily, "But I'll put it outside for a real bird and leave the cage door open." Delia had her own ideas, she worked hard to be different from me.

❏

They had twin boys with deep clefts in their chins. That was Arthur's most obvious contribution to their inheritance, one of the things of value he left them besides the ability to feel sorrow, something they never appreciated.

Actually, I didn't see much of myself in our only daughter. But she did, because she blamed me for who she was. Reproached me for the fact that she had PMS, that her bread wouldn't rise, that her ears flapped out, that her thighs were puffy, that her teeth defied orthodontia. She thinks it's my fault that her French knots unraveled, she can't balance her checks and can't spell onomatopoeia, even on the third try. She said I had almost ruined her life because I told that non-Euclidian geometry was invented by the devil.

I never thought I would be a good mother. Good mothers were born with immutable acceptance of the double helix. I hoped the cryptic code would not give me more than I could handle. I was afraid of unborn words and the lost nesting needed to deliver them, that the embryo within me would leak before it was ready to come out.

My mom, Rose, whom I loved once or twice, did not understand that my planetary house was not in order. She gave generic consolation, tried her best to comfort me with homeopathic remedies that she ordered from a practitioner in Salt Lake City. Only the black walnut bark capsules worked.

Rose had a mother who criticized her. Her shoes were not properly shined, spots would not come out of her dresses, she fiddled with her hands, stammered when she spoke, and was smarter than her brother. Rose grew up to be an extension of her mother like her fingernails, a part that could be regrown, formed, filed, polished or clipped out of existence. And I, who should have known better, had flowered into the same kind of Rose.

I saw my genetic line going back to pioneer women, all yacking and blaming their moms, everyone forced to relive an indelible pattern they didn't know existed. As women we had been programmed to take care of the needs of others, when what we needed, more than anything, was the comfort of caring for ourselves. Foolishly, I thought motherhood would be, at most, a twenty year job. I didn't know that it was an occupation you could never get quite right, that it would not be completed even when you died; that daughters would take a vow never to be like their mothers, because when they saw their faces in the mirror, they saw their mother's eyes.

Predictably, at a certain age I switched from blaming my mother to blaming Delia.

❑

I remember Delia in her white straw hat, sitting on the sand, a beach towel over her legs as though she was cold. She had nice legs, but whenever I looked at her, she was wearing a towel or something that covered them. She liked to sit down by the water's edge, buried up to her neck in sand. "This feels nice and warm," she said. "At last."

She has cold feet," said Arthur, trudging after sand encrusted children. "My back can tell you that."

I might have known then, that she wasn't well, but I didn't. The last time, years ago, Jon and I visited at the lake, Delia and I had one of our falling outs. "Delia," I began and didn't get further than that.

"Why did you have to give me such a stupid name?" she asked. "'Delia, Delia stinks like a camellia.' Did you know the kids always teased me?"

Why bring that up? "That was grandma's name on your father's side. Anyway, if you don't like it, change it."

"Names, like cockroaches, should not be inherited," she said and off she went to the beach, trailed by the kids.

❑

I walked slowly to her bed. She looked as though she had been eaten by small rabbits. Last year she lost her right leg. It was then that she told us she has Reynaud's disease, a circulatory condition that gnaws on the patient extremities. Now she was losing her left leg.

Delia's hospital room mate near the door was listening to Rockabilly music. It was loud and strong, taking me by force. It covered everything like bug spray and tanning cream, seared memory into gelatinous blobs the size of walnuts.

As I looked at my daughter, far from the water's edge, I remembered visions I had before she was born, thalidomide dreams about flipper babies and the one I had when I was eight months pregnant. I look into the crib and there, to our delight, is Delia at six months sitting up and talking. She climbs over the crib rails, drops to the floor and walks. At a year she's in kindergarten, studying for finals. At ten she's writing a doctoral thesis. Her life rushes faster and faster, accomplishments piling up. As time accelerates, something unsettling begins to happen. The dream shows it to me with immense clarity. At twelve she looks like a mature woman but she's exhausted. By sixteen she is stooped and bent. She dies. I woke up with a shout, dangerous thoughts and feelings shaped themselves. The dream is about my daughter but it is also about me. We are going faster than the speed of light into an empty darkness, where the light bends as it passes and life is a shooting star.

I told her that dream shortly after she married Arthur, a man who could fix everything, including optimism. She had the twins, she was going to night school, president of the PTA, and doing a million other things. "Don't push yourself so hard," I said, trying to use the dream as a warning.

"I'm not surprised," she said. "A typical mother dream. You want me to be an achiever, even though you deny it. You want me to be what you never were."

"Of course. Doesn't every mother want the best for their child? Delia . . . ?"

"Try Dee," she said.

❑

She went home from the hospital Monday. Arthur pushed her in the wheel chair, an item of furniture that she can not redecorate with acrylic paints or bird cage fabrics.

"Daddy called," she said, making her conversation with her father on the cellular phone feel more intimate than the one we were having at the time. Jon usually called from his car, liked that much better than talking in person. The phone was like a huge umbilical cord that tied him to us, a Pavlovian bell we salivated to, and when the gong sounded I turned off my computer, put down my needlepoint, my toothbrush, my free weights, my book — whatever — to answer the call. The telephone was a distancing device, invented by men to give the appearance of being closer, while actually all they had on their minds, was the road.

❑

A month later, after the surgeon removed her left leg, Delia sat in her chair, wearing a flowered skirt, dainty and erect. Her stump was killing her. She didn't want company. She didn't want anyone to see her until she was ready. Arthur carried in a tray with tea and *Lorne Doones* from Ralphs' market. He had put a white paper doily on a tarnished silver serving tray. Small dark hairs grew on the back of his robust fingers. He fussed with the delicate bone china cups, trying to set up everything the way Delia would.

"I'd never buy that store-bought crap," she said eyeing the cookies. "You know that. I still have stuff in the freezer from before I went to the hospital. A couple of mesquite chickens and a bundt cake I'm saving for a special occasion."

I swizzled a lump of sugar into my tea, watching it dissolve into the color of dead rivers. "You'll be able to cook again, soon, Delia. Really, Arthur says you're doing so well. You just need to take your mind off yourself. " I ate two *Lorne Doones*. Arthur was glad to leave the room.

"Damn it, Mom. Can't you stop being sweet? I don't want to be grateful." Delia sighed.

I didn't know what to say. I hated being nice to her, being comforting, being supportive, being careful.

"Hold your pity in check," she said when I left, "I'll call you."

Of course, I was sorry for her. For her pain, for her legs cut off from her body. For my own pain in seeing hers. And they needed money. Arthur had lost his business and along with it, the big house. I never quite understood his problem. But suddenly he was selling furniture at the Broadway in Los Angeles and Delia, who was not able to physically handle large canvasses anymore, concentrated on selling her smaller animal prints.

They moved to a cramped apartment in the San Fernando Valley with an avocado and gold kitchen, wall paper that had been old in the seventies and green shag rugs that showed foot prints. The corridors smelled as though cigar smoking men in undershirts played poker there while they watched video porn. Elephant leaf plants grew in the atrium bending towards the pebbled cement steps begging for a bath. The mail box was rusted shut, and a jumble of letters lay on a small spray painted gold table to the left of the front door. Many of the tenants listed themselves by a first initial and last name, a sure give-away that they were single women and afraid.

❏

Eight months passed. She sat demurely in her chair. She had done a new watercolor series of nocturnal fighting creatures with upside down eyes, night blooming ocelots, cock-a-toos, raccoons and emus, things that want to fly but only fall.

Two ugly and intimidating pink leg prosthesis were at her side. "I'll never wear these damn things," she cried and flung them away from her. With her diminished strength, the legs didn't travel far.

I have a prosthesis smile. I am the cheerful one who can tell everyone else how to live, but can only swim in shallow water.

"Want to see my stumps?" she asked.

If I ever have free time I will wrap myself in an old Navajo Indian blanket adorned with something crusty and suspicious on the sleeve. The only books I will read will be about the lives of serial killers because there is nothing within me that could deal with seeing my daughter being whittled down to nothingness. I didn't want to see the real. I would rather keep it covered up in brown wrapping paper, out of sight in the back of my stocking drawer.

I was pulled back to the present. Delia's little left finger was bandaged. It was a quarter of an inch shorter than the others. "They tipped it," she said. "A nice euphemism for 'hacked.' I'm dying by inches. I can't stand it. Get me something when it gets too bad."

"Delia, I can't hear this kind of thing."

"What kind of mother are you? You bring flowers and send thoughtful cards and then let them carve me up like a God damn turkey and come around here with your God damn cheerful face . . . "

"What can I do?" Nothing will grow new legs from those stumpy buds. She needs a balm for pain and remembrance, something that cures the outward curve of time, that bleaches memory until it seems what happened to someone else, or happened differently. A salve that shapes the air differently, spins the lake into gold. A refillable prescription that tastes like honey laced with *Jack Daniels* and a little formaldehyde.

Who do I know? Who will come? What number to call? I don't want a physician from Harvard. I want a Filipino witch doctor who can put his hand inside her body and pull out chicken hearts. I want voodoo bones, an Australian Aborigine with blonde hair who will grind up a few snakes, a Chinese apothecary who deals in forbidden ivory potions. I want secret remedies that call for eye of newt. I want the remedies for her. I want them for me.

When I was a kid we made special mud pies with gravel, oleander leaves and uncured olives that smashed black on the side walk. We served them with glasses of mud water, laced with rolly polly bugs and fragments of fossil oysters we dug out of the hills in Topanga. We would have put night crawler guts in the brew but nobody had nerve enough to cut up the worms because they might scream. But this we knew, any one who drank our brew was special.

When my mother saw what we were up to in the back yard she flew out the door and yelled like crazy, not because we were actually eating the stuff, mind you, but because my sister and I had dribbled it down our nice white sun dresses.

There is no cure for what ails Delia, Mother Rose. Nothing can touch that vortex, she will sit in solitary confinement, being eaten alive. How can she accomplish anything sitting and doing nothing?

❑

Delia rolled her chair forward as if to dissolve the distance between us. "Get me the right drugs. Find out what it takes."

Suddenly I felt that I was at the condition before possibility. That singular moment of existence before the world was born, zero minus a nano second, when everything converged — like an orchestra at attention before the maestro begins. The conductor has an idea of what can happen, has a hope, has a dream, doesn't know if the musicians are up to it, if the triangles are ready, but he goes ahead and something is born that wasn't there before. Where was the world before it began? First there was absolute nothing and then there was an absolute something.

I tried to tell her my thoughts but all Delia wanted was *Codeine.*

We drank our tea in silence. No more bundt cake left in the freezer, none made. The apartment was dark and sullen, nothing like the light in the house by the lake. I left like an angry cat.

❑

Three months later. Another finger tipped. No sign of the prosthesis. She was wearing a long, billowing denim skirt. I could almost make myself believe she had legs.

"You look better," I lied. I have never had a problem with untruths, different versions of reality to stitch in the moment. Perhaps I learned as a child that when the punishment doesn't fit the crime, you must adjust the crime.

I remember my father's big hand coming down on me, hitting me. His big hand came down from the mountain like Moses when I was bad, when I told something untrue. He demanded submission. "I'll never lie again," I lied.

"Arthur," I asked when we had a moment alone. "What's happening?"

"The doctors think she's stabilized now. She should be all right for a while. She wants you to help her sell her drawings but she's not going to ask you."

One day I came over and she handed me her newest portfolio. "Mom," she said quietly, in that wispy voice covered in honey, but prickly, nonetheless. "I don't know if I'm up to this. Here's a list of leads. People who have bought from me before."

She sat up a little straighter then, handed me her work, and wheeled herself to her desk, then turned her chair around to face me. "Mom, did you know that inside me is a fiftyish, gray haired woman with hair dyed blonde? Someone who has to get up to go to the bathroom in the middle of the night? Someone who recycles unused gifts and used gift wrap? Someone who loves Victorian bird cages."

"I don't know if I go for that theory," I said, "but if it's true, then how about vice-versa. There's a part of you inside me? Doesn't it work both ways?" I smiled, warming at her unexpected feelings.

"Of course, and that's the damnedest thing of all. Inside you there used to be a wild young woman with long black hair wearing teeny cut off shorts, bra-less beneath her T shirt, driving a jeep, who won't take shit from anyone. But I haven't seen her much lately."

"Neither have I, Dee. Neither have I."

"It's really OK. You did the best you could. Everyone does."

She flashes me a knowing smile, as though something has clicked in her head, as though she understands the passage of light that bends when it leaves the universe, as though she can reach out and touch the edge of the galaxy, that she can speak the language of thousand year old sea turtles, that she can ride night blooming ocelots and all the things that want to fly without falling. She knows that time has no value except as a commodity, something to use up every day like soap. Delia is out there on the high wire, balancing herself without a parasol.

Light bends when it passes, illluminating us with its grace. And I know, now, that to think about the lake is to know a time when Delia and I gave the appearance of being whole. ❑

Phoebe Frank
© 1996

Once I had time, now time has me.

Quadrant G

I HAD HEARD MIXED REVIEWS ABOUT QUADRANT G ever since I was a child. My father said he would never stay there overnight; my mother said it sounded quite nice. Quadrant G was one of many Los Angeles governmentalities developed by the city in 2098. Each quadrant was like a tiny city-state, each designated by different letter of the alphabet, each with its own raison dêtre. Quadrant G was administered by the Girl Scouts of America, a corporation that had been awarded its own governmentality by demonstrating it could eat the Boy Scouts for breakfast.

Nobody I knew had ever been to Quadrant G, though every citizen was required to go once a year. The whole idea of G was, **Be Clean, Be Nice, Or Else.** G handled administrative duties about stuff none of the other quadrants bothered with; back-and-forward taxes, credit records, your health, your dog and driver's license renewal, and your Girl Scout Cookie debts. G was the place of reckoning, the central hub through which all citizens must pass, and since everyone was required by law to do it, avoiding G was one of our chief pastimes.

To dodge G, you went to the G SQUAD representative in your home quadrant to get a courier to bring your papers into and out of Quadrant G to obtain the official stamps.

The lines into Quadrant G were so long that you could not be seen every year, but for a price you could be advanced in line, or change your yearly requirement to a less hectic biennial schedule. When you died, you had to give up your number in line, and computer clerks were never surprised to have a citizens' papers submitted fifty years too late (or too early). Selling places in line was a good source of income.

The sticky fact is I had to go to Quadrant G because of my Girl Scout Cookie debt, and this was a most serious offense. For the past ten years, during the three months of cookie season, I had been receiving my quota of the Scout's goodies, as required by law, but I had never eaten one, nor paid for a single box. It's not that I didn't want to eat those cookies. I dreamed of them at night, imagining *Thin Mint* chocolate goodies sliding down my throat, the feel of peanutbutter on the middle tongue. But I did not want to become enslaved to them as most other people were. So I fed them to the ducks who grew too fat to fly further south than my neighbor's lawn. They made HUGE duck patties on the lake, which raised the level of pollutants in the water, which required draining, which raised our taxes, much to the delight of Quadrant G.

You could order any kind of cookie you liked in theory, but in practice ordinary people never saw the fabled *Thin Mints.* Being scarce, there was a brisk Black Cookie Market on *Mints,* and a glut of *Shortbreads.* Your order was delivered by chattering little girls in green. If you wanted more than your quota, you could buy them in front of any Supermarket, but only infrequently could you catch a glimpse of the legendary *Thin Mints* being eaten behind smoked glass in chauffered limousines.

What you owed on your cookie debt was computed in Quardrant G, and the debt was automatically deducted yearly from your bank account..But due to some some flubbox in the computer, (and the fact that my name is Tammy Zachs) I had never once paid my cookie bills. Z's were a *de facto* protected species.

My GPER had to carry papers, which were not papers at all, but a microchip card with all my vital statistics on it. You merely had to identify yourself as the holder of the card (regardless of whether your picture and your actual personage matched). It was one of the few things that made complete sense in our governmental system.

The adjacent downtown area, except for the spotless Quadrant G, was encased in a kind of urban sludge. The bright colors of indecipherable gang logos all melded into a brown piddle.

There was no more heinous crime than cheating on your cookie bill, although some people thought that murder of a Girl Scout Commander might be one. The Scout's organization having fostered addiction by the simple action of withholding its products, could foment chocolate rage and peanutbutter deprivation in the populace. By not eating their cookies, I had remained beyond their maniuplation. Until now.

The Scout's organization took care of their own, in ways that were secretive and strange, but damned effective. In Quadrant G, Girl Scout Cookie Season was celebrated all year long, not just for three months. The little girls in green got no time off for good behavior. You could find them clicking their sharp little pointed teeth, shivering in winter, dripping wet in springtime or boiling in the summer. They stood on street corners, in front of supermarkets and gas stations, their little knees knocking, and their little mouths burbling, "Please, oh please Sir, have pity and buy a hundred boxes." Their mothers, like the ducks, grew fat from the cookies, and stood nibbling the sample stock on tables next to their daughters, praying to the Cookie God that their daughters would fill their quotas so that the whole family would not go to prison.

Each Girl Scout in each Troop, whether a Brownie or a Senior Scout, had her quota. Each troop in each quadrant had its quota; so did each city and country. The quotas were over and above what was assigned to each citizen by law. For three months of the year—except for Quadrant G, where there was no respite—mothers and daughters arose at 5 AM, going over their cookie lists, and leads, and planned their cookie campaigns.

The quotas could have been easily satisfied, had there been a decent supply of *Thin Mints*. Everyone said they would have sold out in a nanosecond. My grandmother had left me a ten year old box of *Thin Mints* in her will, and they were still edible, so I know they existed, although some said the *Mints* were *Fig Newtons* of the imagination. So, little green girls fell asleep on their school buses clutching their cookies with tired little fingers. Sometimes, as they dazedly pursued their prospects, they stumbled into wells. If they were lucky enough to have *Thin Mints*, they made excellent flotation devices, but most, like *Peanut Butter Sandwiches* dragged them down, and the children dropped to the bottom of the well still clutching their cookie boxes.

Usually, however, the little girls could shake off sleep long enough to hunt down their quarries, though some of their prey tried to hide behind trees, jump from second-story windows, or join the Witness Protection Program. The little green girls with their sharp little teeth always had a pencil ready for the customer to sign their order forms. And their little mouths made dainty sucking sounds when they got home and told their mothers.

I had once sold cookies, too, and I knew the terror of the 5 AM wake-up call, when the leads led to nothing, and the morning madness was upon my mother and me. The only thing that fathers had to do was pay up and eat the cookies, or give them to their buddies at the hardware store, where men who were admiring tools could munch *Shortbreads.* They never suspected that such things as *Thin Mints* existed, because men in the hardware stores and bowling alleys usually ate whatever was put in front of them without question.

Once or twice I had not sold my quota, and there are still demerits on my soul. I barely escaped going to Girl Scout prison where they forced you to learn the G language, which paralleled English, except that you had to substitute a g at the beginning of each noun, while putting gs on verbs, adjectives and adverbs earned you more points. *A gase in goint.* A case in point, it was a diabolically clever punishment because it destroyed all useful communication, which was of course, the whole idea. If you said, "Goddamn it, you gon-of-a-gitch, guck you," your message lost much of its charm. Once you learned G language, you could never escape from it completely. It was like a dialect in that no matter how hard you worked to erase it, remnants of G language would pop out of your mouth at the garndest moments, letting everyone know you had once failed.

No matter how high the mighty might rise, G language could bring them down.

I escaped Girl Scout Prison by the only way possible; I agreed to up my personal cookie quota. So now, mom and I had merely to arise at 4 A.M..

As you can see, I was no stranger to offense. I had a quirky personality at odds with everyone else. I wore *Badger Black* nail polish long before it was popular. When I got up in the morning it took me until 11 PM to feel cheerful and by then it was too late. My lips had not learned to laugh, my brow was freeze dried in a frown. Though I never ate them, I lusted for cookies in my heart in a way that makes gluttony look like casual indifference. *Girl Scout Cookies* were the foundation of my soul, and the structure of my being, and I knew that one taste would lead to damnation.

Although I hoped to be in and out in a matter of hours, I booked a room in Quadrant G's *Caramel Delight Inn*. I had hired a GPER Supervisor to clear the way for me. You might have expected to pay an exorbitant fee for a GPER, but actually, the payment was in the form of service because money wasn't very useful to us, since it took so much time to actually spend it. No one had time enough to do anything in our world, where everything traveled at the speed of light.

But stop to think about it for a moment. If everything travels at the speed of light, and nothing is stationary, then everything appears to stand still and go no place. The closest I can come to explaining the cosmic glue that gummed up everything is comparing it to the olden days, in the 1990s. You may think satellites beaming hundreds of television stations increased the number of programs we saw, but quite the reverse, by the year 2000, not one in twenty people ever saw a complete show in the eight o'clock hour. It began to dawn on people that the faster they went, the slower they became, in mind and body.

People have no time to perform their own simple maintenance functions. Not only because everything went by too fast to be counted, but because much of our time was taken up with the selling, buying and eating of *Girl Scout Cookies.* The most effective bribe for a GPER was a postage stamp, or a box of tissues. A sample bottle of shampoo or conditioner from the Caramel could work wonders with the Girl Scout interviewer. The biggest bribe was to offer to stand in line for them when their own G Quadrant notice appeared.

G Quadrant was, when compared to the other quadrants, depressingly clean. And brown. And green. (The colors of the Girl Scout uniforms). It was not only the trees and foliage that were green, it was that the color green (the same faded hue of the Girl Scout uniform) was everywhere. All the windows in G Quadrant were in the shape of big green or brown buttons, and they marched smartly up and down the facades of the buildings. And people smiled at you and were cheerful and did their best, even when they were swindling you. If Disneyland were run by the Girl Scouts, instead of Mickey Mouse on Main Street, you would see Girl Scouts in huge inflatable costumes, selling you the newest flavor, *Chocolate Fudge Nippies.* "It's a Small World, After All," would only feature Girl Scout Dolls in historical dress, and at the end of the ride they would teach CPR on a Girl Scout life-size mannequin, because you wouldn't want to practice on a real person, would you? Someone with warts and things in his nose?

I arrived early for the appointment that my GPER had arranged. I was going to meet with Sonja Droga, an ex-major in the Russian Army, and current G Quadrant commander. I knew she was an ex-major because she usually referred to herself in the third person. Droga had a face the color of *Peanut Butter Patties*, a tawny yellow gold. A platter of *Strawberry Creams* sat on her desk, with a few broken pieces of *Thin Mints* scattered in among them. I felt my hives rising. My tongue felt tense. When Droga looked at me, I thought she was not seeing me, but my rancid account. I told her how amazed I was at the cleanliness of this sector. The people looked like they had been scrubbed regularly (and possibly dipped in a cleaning solution). No patches on the jeans, no holes in the stockings, no lipstick stains.

"How do you do it?" I asked.

"You remember Singapore in the nineties?" she asked, holding her thighs closely together in case something might fly in.

"Well, I do remember they had some pretty severe punishments when their rules were broken," I said. "Is that what you do here?"

"We have our ways." Her voice was stiff as a starched collar. Her merit badges, dipped in chocolate, were lined up smartly on her desk.

Whats this *gedal* for? I asked, slipping into G language. I hoped she hadn't noticed. After all, I was trying to be polite.

"Number of boxes of cookies ex-major Droga sold."

"And this one?"

"Numbers of deadbeats ex-major Droga made pay up."

I should have stopped there, but it was too late now.

"And this one?"

"Number of people ex-major Droga converted to our ways. You will be one of them."

"I see." But I didn't. "When you say, converted to our ways, what do you mean?"

"The Girl Scout Promise, you remember is 'On my honor I promise to do my best for God and my country.' Well, the motto of Quadrant G is **'Be Clean, Be Nice, Or Else.'**"

"Or else what?" I dared ask.

"We have a system that makes the crime fit the punishment. Now, lets get down to your case, shall we? It says on your file you have NEVER paid up your cookie bill, and that you don't eat Girl Scout Cookies. You owe several thousand dollars in back payments, plus interest. We cannot allow this deviant behavior. You are a bad example to your neighbors and little girls standing on street corners all around the country." She took my microchip identity card, swiped it through a bank computer terminal and said, "There, I've withdrawn the proper amount from your bank."

I didn't have enough money in my account to pay my bill and told her so.

Major Droga was unfazed. "You'll get it," she said, "Or Else."

I was not all that worried about paying, since my cookie debt was merged with all my other ones. We all went through the motions of paying, but since everything was going at the speed of light, in continuous income and outgo, our status at any given moment was unclear. The purpose of meeting Droga was to validate the system and feed my cookie lust. Citizens who understood this tenant did not have to hyperventilate.

"You'll need an attitude adjustment," Droga said, taking a bite of *Strawberry Creams* and licked her lips. "You'll need your demeanor swept, your idiosyncrasies scourged so that your personality chart will fit under the bell shaped curve. Lucky, you're not that tough of a case. One night at *Caramel Delight Inn* should fix you up. In the meantime, I suggest you begin by standing straight. We don't like slumping in the Cookie Sector." Ex-major Droga saw me struggling to compose myself, and opened a pale green file on her desk.

"This is your record." It looked pretty small. "It shows that ever since third grade you have spurned the Scouts."

I gulped.

"Ms. Mattson notes your incomprehension of the yeast rising. The only cookies you claimed not to be allergic to, were from Mrs. Fields," she paused and looked at me with a wicked flicker in her eyes. "You know, don't you, that Mrs. Fields is dead? You were in cookie denial from the beginning. Ms. Sears said that your social skills were woeful." She snapped the folder shut. "That last we could do something about."

I felt dreadful. "How?" I squeaked.

"You want to fit in, don't you? You want to live in a nice clean home, help the schools with the cookie sales. You want to eat your cookies because it's the right thing to do. Isn't that so?" Her mouth made little clicking sounds.

I wanted to leave, but and I know this sounds strange—the

chair wouldnt let me. I felt as though I was in some kind of restraint. Yet I could see nothing unusual about the chair. I did not want to be part of the cookie domain. And yet, not everything about her suggestions were so bad.

"If you cooperate, you might even become a Cookie Queen Mother," ex-Major Droga pointed to a series of glamour photographs of mothers shot through heavy gauze. They all had pasty complexions and eyes that seemed strangely fixated on something in the far horizon. Bright and shining, their lips stretched over taut smiles, fifty years of Cookie Queen Mothers beamed down their gluttony at me.

I was tempted.

Ex-major Droga went to the window and pointed to a large dark brown building built to resemble a huge stack of *Thin Mints*. "Children in Quadrant G learn math facts and social responsibility through practical life experience." She placed a textbook before me. "Look at these math problems." Her breath carried a hint of peanut butter.

I rifled through the pages of text. Every problem was set in cookie terms. If you sold thirty boxes of Girl Scout Cookies at $3.00 each and you lost the money on the way home from the supermarket, what would you do?

"I don't see that as a math problem," I said hopefully.

"The question is not about the answer," she said with a steel glint in her eye. It was the look a butcher sends a turkey just before he gives it the ax. It was executioner's look of triumph when he knew he was not a turkey, when he confirmed for himself he was not fowl.

"The answer is pay up. Do you see," her voice became softer, "how we teach life's little lessons? This is a question about morality, not arithmetic."

I closed the book. I could imagine all those bright and shining children learning about life in terms of boxes sold and unsold, trying to figure out how much sugar per batch, trying do their best for cookie shelf life, God, the yeast and the Girl Scouts. Or Else.

"That about does it for today," she said. "Ex-major Droga expects to see you at nine tomorrow for your last session. Dr. Baker will do your psychological survey." Droga leaned forward menacingly, "Ex-major Droga doesn't want your test results to show any abnormalities, and neither do you."

Oh, oh. I hadn't realized I'd have to take the mental status exam.

"I expect after a good night's sleep at the *Inn*, that you'll fit smoothly under the bell shaped curve. That's what we expect here in Quadrant G. No blemishes. No broken, substandard pieces. All your standard deviations will be flat. We like to say here in the Cookie Sector, a good line is a flat line."

I felt the chair release me.

❑

Olive Maroon showed me to my room at the *Caramel Delight Inn*. "Miss Zachs," she said, with an edge of contempt, "Don't sit on the bedspread." The sign on the wall said the same thing.

Olive Maroon put my overnight case on portable luggage stand. "There's ten percent off in the gift shop on all green Girl Scout shirts. There's a thirty percent surcharge for every box of cookies used from your bedside table or closet." she said.

Strange she said "used."

Olive Maroon gestured toward the closet which was packed full of cookies, as though she was demonstrating where the oxygen is on an airplane in case of emergency. "Don't put no suitcases on the bed, neither."

Other strategically placed reminders were all about the room —*Do not talk to the television after 10 P.M.* Why would you want to talk to the TV at any hour? Who were the people that did, and what had happened to them?

Olive Maroon stood next to my case, as though trying to divine its inner contents. "You got a hair dryer in there?"

"Yes, why?"

"It won't kill anything, you know," she said. "Call the desk if you want something." She slammed the door and I noticed the sign on the back of the door—*No slamming, please.*

I opened the bathroom door and the odor of deoderizer, *Authentic Cookie Aroma* spray assaulted me. The white strip of paper across the toilet seat said—*Remove Before Using.* It would be next to impossible to sit on the toilet without removing the warning to remove the paper.

Plastic glasses, terrycloth towels and painfully thin slabs of soap, as substantial as communion wavers, sat by the side of the sink. I thought I could make points if I brought Droga a few samples of hair conditioner and shampoo.

Please do not water anything else—said a sign to the left of the cold water faucet. The only possible thing to water was the dusty plastic rose on top of the dresser.

❑

I had forgotten to take something to read and turned to the *Girl Scout Cookie Bible as Told by Famous Talk Show Hosts,* which I found in my bed table. I sat on the bedspread, even though the sign advised not to in the strongest possible lettering. I propped a pillow up behind me, and tried to read. I had the strangest sensation that the bedspread did not like being sat on. Every now and then I looked at it. The bedspread design was a loose network of wriggling leaves and vines that choked each other against a pale chartreuse background. The ragged plants looked as though they had been chewed into lace doilies, devoured by insects. My eyes began to close, I had had a tiring day. A dish of *Shortbread* cookies stood waiting on the table, along with a cold glass of milk. My hives itched. My desire rose. A bottomless hunger it was, too. I could imagine cookie molecules dissolving on my tongue, my mouth salivating. The glorious taste of fat, sugar and butter coating my throat. I vowed not to give in.

As I sat on the bed it felt as though the vines on the bedspread moved beneath me, just the slightest pressure, a sensation like raindrops hitting earth, or flies landing on a cake.

I read for quite a while. Finally, my eyes closed, the cookbook fell to the floor, and I fell asleep, fully dressed. I imagined sinewy tendrils encircling me. I awoke with a start at 1 AM; the dull light illuminated the bedspread. The number of vines and plants in the design had multiplied. I did not want to fall back asleep so I got up, undressed, did the usual night things, tried to remove the coverlet, but it seemed to be sewn in place. I got under the covers, and even though I had left the light on, against my will, my eyes closed and soon the bedspread was on the march again. I felt a soft, warm pressure; gentle as the tips of peacock feathers, something moving along the surface of the covers up and over my body toward the plate of cookies.

I opened my eyes. The design did not like to be seen moving. As long as my eyes were open I could control the movements of the spread. The plate of *Shortbreads* was empty. I knew I hadn't eaten them. I opened the bottom bedside table drawer, found a stash of *Chocolate Fudge Nippies* and laid them out on the plate. Then, with almost superhuman effort, I got the coverlet off the bed onto the floor. I took a deep breath, turned out the light, relaxed and fell asleep.

Some time later, I awoke to see the vines had flowed off the bedspread and eaten almost all the *Nippies* on the plate. When the light was on, the bedspread shrank back, quivering as though there was a breeze in the room. I got up, took a step forward. The vines, leaves and flowers reformed themselves into a flat and static pattern. I came nearer, bending down to look more closely at the maw of the florid blossoms and I touched one with my finger. Immediately I felt a tiny prick, like the bite of a mosquito and a drop of rosy fluid rose at the tip of my finger. The mouth of the flower turned scarlet with my blood and made little green clicking sounds.

I drew my hand away and jumped back, the crimson spot at the center of the blossom slowly absorbed into the cover, the petals closed in as though they were drinking. I ran to the door but could not open it, I tried breaking a window with a chair, but the glass would not break, and the impact made no sound. I thought of trying to kill the bedspread with my hair dryer, but I remembered Olive Maroon's warning that hair dryers can't kill anything. I called her on the *Inn's* phone, but all I got was an automatic telephone voice mail that gave me a cookie menu in three languages. The only thing on TV was a picture of Mrs. Fields, stripped naked, chained to a stove. At least she was not dead. It was past 2 PM and I was talking to the TV, even though the sign said not to.

I vowed to stay up all night, but again my eyes closed and I dreamt I was trying to kill a big, ugly black water bug. I tried to drown it in a glass of water. I blasted it with my hair dryer, which, inexplicably had become a flame thrower. I hit it with a rolled up magazine and it splattered something pasty like the Girl Scout in sandwich cookies, white frosting on the paper. I threw it in a metal waste paper basket. I had killed it dead all right, but I dreamed that all night long I heard it scratching against the container, trying to get out. When I looked at it to make sure it was dead, it had the face of ex-major Droga. "Gucking gitch," it said.

I awoke from this nightmare and ran to the bathroom. I glanced at the mirror and saw I had a wild look and dark circles around my eyes. I turned on all the lights and watched the bedspread binging on *Chocolate Fudge Nippies.* I took out more cookie boxes from the closet and all night long fed the bedspread. Finally just for comfort, just this once, I ate one, too. Then another and another; all night long I ate vats of cookies.

In the slippery morning sunlight, the quilt stopped its orgy.

❑

I returned next morning to Quadrant G headquarters in a different mood, I was standing straighter. I was cheerful. I was wearing a new green blouse purchased in the hotel gift shop. Ex-Major Droga looked at me with satisfaction when I gave her a miniature bottle of shampoo and conditioner.

"Ex-Major Droga wants you to meet Dr. Baker," she explained. "Just answer these questions for your mental status report."

Baker, a small woman with thick set eyes put the cold papers down in front of me. All the problems were set in cookie terms. The first one was:

> If you sold thirty boxes of Girl Scout Cookies at $3.00 each and you lost the money on the way home from the supermarket, what would you do?

Thank God, I knew the answer. "Pay Up," I said with confidence. " Or else." From there on it was easy sledding.

When I was finished, Dr. Baker graded my psychological exam right there. Ex-major Droga munched on *Thin Mints.* When she opened the door to a small anteroom, I could see hundreds of boxes stored there.

"Well, Doctor, how did she do?" Droga asked when the doctor finished grading my test results.

Baker reached for a *Chocolate Fudge Nippie* and a double helping of *Thin Mints.* "Just fine," he said. "All her lines are flat."

The ex-major looked at me with a smile of satisfication and passed me the plate of cookies. *"Want a Thin Gint?"* she asked, and I took a handful.

It was time to go home.

❑

Computer Talk

The computer's instant thousand eyes
Analyzed data that the young man fed it.
Its binary corpuscles flashed an answer with
Almost human pride.

"It's very scientific," the young man said,
Gazing at the screen.
"We can measure light.
It travels 186,000 miles per second."

"Coming and going?" the woman asked.
"Yes, quite.
We can take the temperature on Mars,
And spectroscope the moon and very soon we'll know
If Venus has an afternoon."

She only said, "Oh."

"We may observe the double helix
Twisted chains,
The way DNA molecules arrange themselves,
Then rearrange.
The secrets in a primordial cell,
We know these kinds of things quite well."

"It really is quite wonderful," she said,
"The way you figure everything on a computer.
But who knows where the light goes,
And why we're here,
And who you are — or for that matter,
Me.
And shall I live another life,
Or if there's God beyond the sky,
Or whom I shall love,
Or when will I die?"

She kissed him lightly on the nose,
And giggled as his spirits rose,
And thought,
The computer age may be terrific,
But not everything is scientific.

❑

A List with My Name on It

HE STOOD AT MY FRONT DOOR and with a toothy grin handed me his business card:

LASZLO WOLFF, M.D.

PROFESSOR OF PSYCHIATRY

UNIVERSITY OF BUDAPEST

I studied the man. He might have been handsome save for the bad tailoring and a slight gap between his two front teeth.

The man smiled, and his eyes danced with excitement. He was tall and slender with prominent cheekbones and silvery white hair. There was a knot of broken blood vessels high on his right temple, and the vague outline of a jagged scar cruised above his brow.

His smile was expectant as though, if given enough time to collect my thoughts, I would surely recall him. "Dr. Guissemar, I'm here at last. Don't you remember me? I'm Wolff, Laszlo Wolff. Here, you gave me this." And with that he showed me a business card with my name on it. The ink had faded, and the corners were bent. The engraved letters of my name had been worn smooth, as though the words had been touched many times.

Still I had no idea who the man on my doorstep might be. As he saw me struggle to recall him, the glow in his eyes began to flicker, and his happy grin was replaced by perplexity. His English had a kind of foreign politeness to it. "We met at Friday night services at the Dohany Synagogue in Budapest last year."

"Ah, yes," I said, trying to part the veil of memory.

"Shabbos," he said, hopefulness flooding his face once more. "We had a nice chat, and you invited me to see you when I came to California. I made a list of everyone to visit — all my American friends." He pulled out a small, worn address book, and flipped the pages to my name.

I had been on a tour of Budapest last summer and I recalled our group's visit to the synagogue, but the faces of the people I met there were a blur. "Well," I said, flustered, "Please, do come in. Yes, I'm beginning to remember now."   Maybe.

The man in the shiny suit followed me out of the marble foyer, past the living room and into my den. He stepped on the deep-piled beige carpet gingerly, as if it were hot to the touch, and gazed at the oil paintings with respect.

"Won't you sit down, Dr. Wolff?" I showed him to a comfortable leather chair, but he planted himself stiffly on its edge.

"Your home is quite beautiful," he said as though he were looking for a way to start the conversation. I thanked him for the compliment but finally admitted that I couldn't quite recollect the circumstances of our meeting.

Dr. Wolff's eyes flicked from the paintings to the books on the coffee table like an anxious bird assessing unfamiliar surroundings. He had looked for a comfortable landing place but now he was not quite sure he had found it.

"Of course, it's hard for you to recall," he said. "You met many people — still I took the chance you might remember."

"Ah, my dear Dr. Wolff, please relax. I'm flattered that **you** remembered **me**. I have no pressing plans for this afternoon. Let's have a glass of sherry." And although he demurred, I poured some in a crystal goblet and put a tray of crackers on the table before him. I watched the man as he sipped his drink and nibbled crackers, and memories began to return.

At first, I thought he might have been the slender man I had encountered a block away from the Dohany Synagogue. *"Gut Shabbos,"* he had said in Yiddish and I returned the greeting. "Are you going to services?" I nodded yes and he fell into step with me. As we continued, the early evening sun dappled the trees. Other early arrivals walked purposefully toward the building that sat like an enormous neo-classical pastry on the corner of the street.

When we reached the steps, my guide suddenly pulled up his sleeve to reveal a tattooed number on his skinny arm. *"Ich war in Auschwitz,"* he said and the look in his eyes pierced my soul. He paused to allow the moment to sink in. "Can you spare some change?" he asked, not unaware of the effect he had on me. I gave him a few loose *forint* from my purse and he tipped his cap. "They're laying the foundation for a memorial to the martyrs in the central courtyard," he said. "More than forty years after the war. A little late, perhaps — have you seen it?"

I told him I hadn't, and he said that sometimes he was hired to guard the memorial and adjacent cemetery at night. It was not a frightening place. The spirits of the dead were finally at rest and nothing more could happen to them. But what haunted him was that the date of death on every tombstone was the same: 1945. All murdered the same year, resting in mass graves in the courtyard, permanently enshrined in shadow.

We had reached the top of the steps and as we went in to the building, the frail man turned and stood blinking in the muted light of the interior. Again he asked for money. He seemed confused, perhaps trying to remember whether or not I had already given him something. I gave him more coins, knowing there were other things he had not forgotten. Then he turned around and went back outside.

No, I thought. That man could not be Wolff.

The synagogue's large, elaborate interior was flanked by a wall-to-wall, double-tiered balcony. Underneath the balcony, the walls were dressed in fine, dark woods. Two tall, intricately worked, filigreed metal candelabra flanked the *bima*, or dais. The floor was a carpet of stone mosaics smoothed by time.

It was quite early, and the congregation leaders, who were acting as ushers, were just putting out the prayer books. They all had the same look I had seen in the eyes of the man who had just walked with me. I had peered into a cauldron of smoking remnants, a bottomless well of crystalline tears, a pool of ineffable sadness, and I was afraid to look too deeply.

The men were all in their sixties, seventies and even eighties. Judaism in the Eastern bloc countries of Rumania, Hungary and Czechoslovakia had become an old man's club. And like the ancient Torahs in the ark, they leaned on each other for support.

I had arrived well before the others in my travel group. I was standing alone in back of the vast sanctuary, when one of the ushers, a distinguished-looking man of about sixty, greeted me. He had strong, well-proportioned features, a milky skin and stark, white hair. The veins in his forehead stood out in a cluster above his right eye, and the white-lined traces of a jagged scar left a ghostly imprint on his face.

Suddenly the kaleidoscope of fragmented memories clicked into focus. That was Dr. Laszlo Wolff!

"Welcome. Welcome." Dr. Wolff had introduced himself and told me about the synagogue. As we moved around the periphery of the sanctuary, he described what had happened to the Jewish community during the war. There were 900,000 Jews in Hungary then. Barely a third of them came back after the war. No longer were there the thousands who had crowded the synagogue on High Holidays

"I'm glad you're here early," Wolff said to me. "We have some Judaica that's worth seeing. Would you care to?" I nodded yes and he took me down a passageway, past a hand-cranked gear mechanism that opened and closed the ark's doors to a small alcove where a locked metal cabinet stood.

We chatted tourist talk while he fumbled for the key. When he found out I was a psychotherapist from Los Angeles, he wanted to know if I lived near Hollywood, and if I had heard of an actress, Monica Breuer. He thought she might have emigrated to the States. She was an old friend, he said wistfully.

"Uhm," was all I said as he rambled on about Monica. When the cabinet was opened I saw a small but beautiful collection of silver candlesticks and wine cups. "Ah, that's like the *kiddush* cup my father used," he said. "And those candlesticks. Just like my aunt's. The war was long ago," he sighed, "But it's still fresh." There was longing on his face as he showed me the silver treasures.

Since services would soon begin, he told me he could arrange for me to see the pieces another time, but I said that our tour would be leaving the next day.

He locked the cabinet once again. As we walked back to the sanctuary, he mentioned he was a Freudian analyst and often worked with Holocaust survivors or their families. "When I treat these people, I see myself in every patient. Do you find that's true, too?"

"Yes," I said. "It seems to be one of the hazards of the trade."

We talked a little bit more and he was interested in my training and areas of specialization. It was then that we exchanged business cards.

"You must come to Beverly Hills and visit me," I said. "I'd be happy to show you around." It was the kind of formula invitation one makes. "Call me, visit me. We'll do lunch." When both parties are women, each smiles and kisses the air near her companion's cheek. Then telephone numbers and addresses are exchanged, and both are thoroughly delighted never to have to meet again.

But apparently Wolff took my invitation more seriously than I had intended. "I should be delighted to see you once more," he said. "I'm coming next year. I finally got all my papers together."

"How long will your visit be?"

"Ah, my dear lady. Forever, of course. It will take a lot of money to finance the trip, but I want to go to the States, no matter what the cost."

"Oh," I said, "How nice." Everyone wants to come to America, I thought. I never expected anyone would show up.

When services started, we had to cut our conversation short. The man was loquacious and friendly and, on impulse, I invited him to join our group for dinner. He accepted with pleasure. We spoke in whispers for a few more moments. Then we separated. He to the men's side, just ahead to the right and slightly in front of me. And me to the left.

The choir, hidden from view somewhere in the balcony above the bima, sang familiar melodies. I tried to get myself to concentrate, but every now and then I'd look up to catch Wolff looking at me. He'd smile shyly and nod. At first I was flattered by his attention, but then I began to think about it.

I'm a reasonably attractive widow of fifty ("financially secure" as they write in the "personals" columns), and I began to suspect that Laszlo saw me as a ticket to Dream City.

The more he smiled at me, the surer I was that I wanted to get out of the dinner invitation I had just extended. He was a charming schmoozer, to be sure, but I didn't want to get involved with him. So when services were over I left before he could find me.

❑

And now he had found me. I refilled our glasses, and Dr. Wolff put a few crackers on his plate. "How long have you been here?" I asked politely.

"A few weeks only. I've started to study for the California License exam, and I've got an offer to teach at UCLA."

I wondered how he could have lined up employment so fast, and he told me, with a slight flush of embarrassment, that he had published several major papers in psychoanalytic journals that had been "rather well received." In fact, he had been corresponding for years with many of the top practitioners in the field, including the Head of UCLA's Department of Psychiatry.

"And Monica has turned up," he said. "Do you remember I told you about her?"

I recalled the name, but not much more.

"Monica — the actress," he said. "I've found her after forty years. I tried to steal her bicycle. That's how it started."

I knew he would tell me the story whether or not I wanted to hear it. And I sat back in my chair, occasionally taking a sip of sherry, to listen.

❑

In 1945, he was living with his parents in Buda. Buda and Pest are twin cities spread across the Danube river, joined together by the graceful Chain Bridge. On the day of the massacre of thousands of Jews in the city, including his family, Laszlo happened to be out of his home. When he came back, he saw all the Jewish tenants from his apartment house lined up on the sidewalk and shot. Then the murdered were picked up and thrown into a wooden cart like garbage.

He was seventeen years old.

Later that same day, the Wolff's apartment was looted by their neighbors, stripped of furniture and everything of value. Gone were the silver candlesticks, the fine china, and the Passover dishes. What the other tenants couldn't carry off, they chopped up with axes, and the quarters looked as if a bomb had gone off within. Along with the apartment, the concept of "home" had been destroyed for Laszlo.

He lived in the street for a day or two, returning only at night to sleep on the floor of the kitchen, but it became increasingly clear that he would have to move on, escape the city.

Directly in back of the Dohany Synagogue was an administration building built around a small courtyard, and one day when Laszlo walked by, he noticed a bike leaning against the wall. A bicycle meant mobility and he decided to steal it.

He was about to try to hack off the lock when he suddenly saw a pair of knobby knees peeking out from a short brown skirt. One little outraged shoe tapped the ground in fury.

He looked up past the skimpy skirt and tight sweater to enormous startled eyes and a small, gaunt face flushed with rage. Her hands darted like ferrets to tuck the falling curls under her beret, to smooth her wrinkled skirt, or pull at the buttons of her shabby sweater. Her name was Monica Breuer, and he was trying to steal her bike. It was love at first sight.

Laszlo was stricken dumb as she continued to tap her foot. Suddenly he understood all the love poems he had ever read, for they were fleshed with reality. An incredible elfin vision with eyes of epic sadness stood in front of him. When she told him her name, he thought it was the most beautiful one he had heard in his life. There was a rhythm to it, a splendid arrangement of sounds and syllables. The name was music in itself. Monica!

She stood nine feet off the ground on the incredible pedestal Laszlo built for her. She looked at him, and for some strange, inexplicable reason — suddenly smiled. He hoped she thought him passable looking, rather than downright ugly.

Then the radiant and enraged Monica opened the bike lock with a tiny key that hung from a scarlet ribbon around her neck. "Take it," was all she said, pointing to the bike. Then, almost as an afterthought, she added, "I'll ride the handle bars."

Laszlo felt as though he had lost his wits and duly followed the girl's commands. The two started forward. She had all the weight of a fly, and, as though it were an ordinary day in ordinary times, the two of them careened down the street laughing.

It seemed to him the sunlight touched the old houses and their baroque ornamentation with a special grace that golden day. Gargoyles smiled from rooftops; statues of musicians lining the facade of the opera house saluted, and sculptures in park fountains gurgled approval.

Soon he grew too tired to pump the bike with both of them and they walked awhile. He couldn't remember when he had last eaten and was sure that it had something to do with his exhaustion.

Eventually, he found out that she was alone, too. In an apartment in Pest. With food! They headed toward it across the Chain Bridge, and he felt as though he were on a magic carpet, flying over the Danube, suspended from the clouds.

He found her every movement adorable. Her tiny feet, her bumptious knees, her anger and her bossiness. Everything she did, every gesture she made was to his liking. She got on the handlebars again and they biked farther into Pest. God had delivered Queen Esther and Bathsheba to him in one delightful package.

He inhaled the aroma of her hair as they rode. The wind riffled it into waves of silk; the sun shone on it and, curiously, made it seem darker and more inaccessible. It flew in his face and brushed his mouth so that he could actually taste the strong soap she used for shampoo.

And although he never could recall the details of what she had said, he thought that everything she spoke about was wonderful and bright. He learned she was an office clerk. She wanted to be an actress, wanted someday to have nylon stockings and a closet full of beautiful clothes in roughly that order. And for some reason, entirely inexplicable to Laszlo Wolff, she wanted him.

Monica took her bike into her apartment, set it against the wall. The room was finer than he had expected a clerk to have. She took out a bit of cheese, jam even, and served something suspiciously like bread. And although it was hard and dry, with an occasional insect baked into it, for him it was as sweet as the honey cake his mother used to make.

Monica poured a weak reincarnation of tea without any signs of feeling nervousness being alone with him. She would be an international film star after the war. She would be rich and famous. Her tiny hands danced in airy gestures, pantomiming a woman smoking a cigarette, and flicked the imaginary ash

toward him. Someday she would be married in the biggest
wedding at the grandest cathedral in Budapest. Her dress
would be designed in Paris. There would be seed pearls on the
bodice and even on the underslip where no one could see them.
But she would know they were there. So she spun her dreams
out to him, her golden fantasies, as though he would under-
stand and care — and enter them with her. For those few
shining moments, the strange, solemn cast disappeared from
her eyes.

But Laszlo had ceased hearing her when she pronounced the
word "cathedral." She was Catholic! He had just assumed she
was Jewish because he had met her in back of the synagogue.
Suddenly his legs were puny supports that could barely hold
him, and his tongue was welded to the roof of his mouth. For
just as Laszlo had allowed himself to be transported into her
visionary world, caught up in the fantasy of her future life —
just as the humble walls around him had become nobly en-
hanced with exquisite paintings, and the faded lace curtains
were replaced with the rich damask of dreams — the scene
cracked and the war returned.

She saw his look of pain and asked him what was wrong. He
had learned you could not trust the *goyim*; they would kill you
or sell you to the Nazis for a crust of bread or a pair of those
stockings that Monica so coveted. And now Laszlo was faced
with the problem of whether or not to reveal that he was a Jew.
Though his brain shouted warnings, the words from his heart
tumbled out and he told her the truth.

She merely shrugged and said nothing.

"I thought you were Jewish," he said. "You were in the courtyard of the synagogue."

And then she told him she worked in the Eichmann office on the third floor of the synagogue's administration building. Lazlo trembled just to think of Eichmann's cruel choice of a synagogue for his office. A shiver of terror raced round in his brain. Eichmann, the chief executor of the Fuhrer's will! And Monica said it so casually, as if she were simply hanging laundry out to dry.

She hated her job, she said. What with having to prepare those lists all day. She was a two-finger typist, and it was hard to get all the numbers and letters just right. And there was such a lot of pressure to work faster, and overtime even. And she didn't get paid much for it. And the room was so hot; not a breeze entered from the courtyard outside. It wasn't her idea to work there. She had been ordered.

Wild thoughts raced through his mind that he dared not share. What kind of lists were they? He could guess what they were for. Whatever they were, he needed to find a way to get copies to the underground. They might save lives.

The tea was finished, and the two sat watching the darkness creep into the room. Neither made a move to turn on the lights. They sat, not saying anything, enveloped by the gathering darkness.

Laszlo had never gone to bed with a woman, and although he had read about it, fantasized it, the reality that it could happen tonight — would in fact happen, could not be stopped from happening — propelled him to reach across the table for her hand.

He could feel the pulse beating rapidly in her wrist. Her fingers were soft and pliable, slightly cool to the touch. She rose from her chair, approached Laszlo and settled into his lap as if she had known him always. Then she put her arms around his neck and kissed him softly on the mouth.

The hairs on the back of his neck stood up and his scalp tingled as the shock waves of her being floated through him. He felt as if he were already flooding into her. Enveloped in her warmth, he sensed himself stiffening, and he worried that she might notice his hardness as it swelled beneath her tiny skirt. And she must have been aware of it, because she put her hand right there on top of his bulging trousers and caressed him. And with every stroke, the strength of his desire grew, demolishing every cautionary inhibition. Every reason, every teaching, every admonition, every demand not to touch a *shiksa* was swept away by the force of his need to have her. From that point, there were no boundaries between them; the evening was ripe with untold possibilities. And then his solemn eyes surrendered to her.

❑

The next morning he awoke under heavy linen sheets topped by a down comforter. He threw back the quilt just as he had done when he was a boy. In fact, for just a moment he thought he was back home, listening to the clink of china as his mother made breakfast. But the rapturous dream broke when he opened his eyes and Monica padded into the bedroom with a hot cup of pallid tea and a small square of chocolate. This time, he decided, reality was better than fantasy.

Wondering what miracles this angel had performed to find such a rare item, he asked about it and learned that Hans had given it to her.

"Hans?"

"Oh, just a friend," she told him. "He means nothing except a way to live a little bit better. Don't worry. He's an officer at the front."

My God! He had had Hans' chocolate as well as his woman. And not only was it his chocolate and his woman, this was his apartment. But Monica smiled sweetly. "We survive as we can."

Laszlo was so shaken he pulled the cover back over his head, hoping Monica would not see him tremble. After Monica left for work, he paced her apartment all morning, trying to figure a way to escape the city. Toward afternoon he crept home to his parents' flat to think. He decided that he would leave that very night. But when he met Monica at her apartment, he could not carry out his resolve. Even when the midnight sweats came upon him and creeping terror gripped him by the neck, he could not command himself to go. But what if Hans returned?

Monica laughed at his fears. "He'll be away for a long time," she said with no hint of remorse.

Then one evening Laszlo urged his love to come to his parents' place. He had cleaned up one of the bedrooms, found some blankets and discarded linens. It was strangely comforting for him to be there among the ruins. The big square dining room table that could seat sixteen was turned over on its side. One of the legs was charred, as though someone had tried, but failed, to set fire to it. The dining room chairs, high-backed, upholstered in rich burgundy velvet, being easy to cart off, were all gone. The gilt-framed mirror, still hanging in its accustomed spot, was shattered.

The parlor was no better. A sofa was hacked to pieces and lay like a broken corpse across the wooden floor. The Persian rugs had been pulled up, and the floor boards moaned when they were walked on. The three bedrooms had all been thoroughly ransacked, the mattresses slashed, pillows mutilated with their guts hanging out. Someone had urinated in the middle of the floor.

He wanted her to see it. To touch his past with her body. To understand his withered future. He was horrified at the feelings he had for the girl who showed so little understanding of what working in Eichmann's office or having a soldier boyfriend meant. Could anyone be that naive? Or was she just pretending? Or simply blocking out the truth? Still, he could not break his compulsion to be with her. If he continued, he rationalized, he might be able to get his hands on those lists.

She sucked in her breath when they entered his apartment. She seemed to glide through it, expressionless, vapid, as though in transit through a nightmare. Laszlo had placed a few candles about and their flicker set shadows moving on the walls. Hacked up furniture punctured the shadows, and the dining room chandelier tinkled softly as they walked on the bare floors.

"Oh," was all she said. "Oh, oh, oh." Each exclamation was punctuated by a tiny breath as she put her fingers to her lips.

You cannot sensitize a person in a day, he thought. You cannot take all they've known, all they've been told, all they've denied and in one dramatic moment, turn their thinking upside down. He could not plumb her reactions. They were too deep; interior, inner.

❑

The next day Monica brought him the first list.

She thought it might be important. She didn't know exactly what the rosters were for, census probably. "Don't ask too much of me," she said, studying him. Night living had made his face whiter than the lace curtains in the parlor.

"Perhaps I can bring the used carbons next time, maybe you could make out the names." She smiled then, and Laszlo thought she had never looked so pretty. "I'll try to remember to bring them," she promised.

Laszlo was grateful. She began giving him little gifts of names and lists, and he used her to get more information, passing it on to the right places.

She seemed unperturbed that they might be found out. Some supreme faith guided her innocence and the strange belief that she was safe because she was "a good actress." But Laszlo thought her luck was predicated on her ability to use men. Perhaps even Eichmann, but he rolled the thought away from his mind and locked it out.

Laszlo remembered how every time he saw her, he thought it would be the last, and thus each meeting was charged by insecurity and an irrational deepening of his feelings. Then one night, just before they were going to make love, Monica, with a horrible, inept sense of timing, showed him a list from Eichmann's office. It had his name on it. The address was the old apartment, but they would find him soon enough.

❑

He had not told her he was leaving her that last night. But he was sure she knew because when he kissed her for the last time, her eyes regained their sadness. Early the following morning before she arose, he quietly unlocked her bike with the key she kept on the scarlet ribbon and crept away. Had he gone back for a last lingering look he would have seen her sitting up in bed, fully awake with her eyes wide open, listening to him go.

A day later, he was picked up by a patrol and pistol-whipped senseless. The head wound turned brown and crusty and the cuts on his forehead oozed pus for weeks. He was sent to Auschwitz where he found himself in a long line of ragged people. As the queue straggled by, the officer checked each person's name against a master list and some prisoners were sent to the left, some to the right. Scuttlebutt had it that the left was the passage to death, the right life. Others said it was just the opposite. Still others said the doors to life and death were randomly switched. Some said it was good if your name was on the list; others disagreed.

They crawled forward like wretched beetles to the table where names were checked against a tally sheet, and then the one queue became two parallel lines that could not converge.

When Laszlo shuffled forward in line the Commandant found his name on the labor requisition list and sent him off to the right.

And he lived.

❏

Laszlo sighed, still immersed in reverie. After the war, he said, he had returned to Budapest, keeping alive the fantasy that he might see Monica again. He saw her riding bikes, walking in the park. He ran after slender women in ill-fitting jackets and short skirts, only to turn away when they weren't her. He boldly investigated the apartment where she had lived with Hans, but no one knew where she had gone.

Laszlo looked at me as though he had come back from some other time and space, and touched the glass to his lips as though offering a silent toast.

"How did you find her?" I asked, spellbound.

I poured more wine for Laszlo, but it remained untouched as he described what had happened.

"Her picture was in the newspaper the first day I arrived here in Los Angeles. It was her face, older of course. But still beautiful, almost as I remembered her. But she has a different name. Nicole Argon. How like Monica to choose such a name; a bit stagey and mysterious. She lived in Hungary until the revolution, and somehow escaped to the United States. She came to Hollywood to become the famous star she always wanted to be."

"Nicole Argon?" Of course I knew the name. She was a wonderful actress, not a superstar, but an important lesser luminary whose memoirs had just been published.

"I've read her story," I said, rummaging through the pile of books on the coffee table to find my copy. "Here it is. I had no idea."

"Perhaps you remember the chapter about Avram?"

"Avram? The man she fell in love with during the war?" And the truth dawned on me. "That was you!"

"Of course! Disguised to a certain extent. Some facts were changed. She made me better looking than I am." He laughed for the first time that afternoon. "And she'd never admit to having a Nazi lover, but otherwise most of the rest is true."

"Have you seen her?" I asked, reeling with this information. To think that Wolff was a personal friend of this movie star! And had been portrayed in her best-selling autobiography, *Danube Memoirs*.

"Yes, of course. I'm living in her home temporarily — she graciously lent me her car so I could visit all the people on my list." He took his address book out again and placed a check mark next to my name. "I didn't mean to go on for so long. Sometimes I lose track," my guest said. "But so many memories have been stirred up. You were kind to listen. I hope I haven't taken too much of your time."

"On the contrary, I'm delighted you came." I was grateful he hadn't mentioned how I'd once weaseled out of dinner. I assured Laszlo it was a pleasure to have seen him once more, and he promised to call me again.

"It's a new life in America," he said as he kissed my hand.

I waved good-bye as he stepped into a Silver Shadow Rolls. A smartly attired driver in a navy blue suit opened his door. I was red with embarrassment, remembering how, when we were in Budapest, I worried that he was going to ask me to help get him to the States, or give him money. At the very least, I had feared he would become a time-consuming project. I had really not wanted to be bothered with him.

❑

I never heard from Laszlo again, although I sometimes read about him in the newspaper. On the social scene, he flits with Nicole from one "A" party to the next. Professionally, he has become quite well known for his controversial psychoanalytic work on the "Survivor Syndrome."

I've often thought about Laszlo's visit. And the aspect of it that haunts me is not why he came, or what he wanted, but that you never know whose list your name might be on.

❑

Origins of Kashrut According to Rabbi Nachman Brachman of Bratloff
A Story Without Any "E"s.

IN DAYS OF OLD, A RAMBUNCTIOUS KNIGHT, SIR IRVING TOLIVAR, saw a grand looking young woman, with upward mounding bossoms, riding ignominiously on a giant pig.

"Why do you sit upon such an absurd animal?" Tolivar did ask.

"In truth, my Lord, I am Lady Gwynn. Our mad King Arthur forbids us all to say or own anything that contains a particular outlaw sound which I can only hint at.

"Most odd," thought Tolivar, instantly ablush, wishing to crawl out of his armor toward Lady Gwynn's twin pillows.

"King Arthur limits my daily toils—only a *milchig* lunch of *matzah*, fish, fruit, lamb and milk. So monotonous! I can don a gown and a chastity strap. I shall jump from thirty-two to thirty-four on my birthday. I cry nightly, trying to pick my words with inhibition so as not to go against King Arthur's laws. Alas, King Arthur wants my hand."

"My God, I will slay this unfair king. His will is immoral, and I will not allow him to constrict your living so. I shall kill him by cutting off his manhood, and thus win your charms, for I hold you in high honor."

"Sir Irving, I would marry you without a qualm. King Arthur did dispatch my last husband for mouthing off and now I cannot find a man who would fight our King. But most important, I am looking for a husband to bring a modicum of physical satisfaction to my boudoir. Finding him, I would shout all kinds of things now in prohibition."

Boldly, Tolivar, visor up, pauldrons rising, sought a kiss from Gwynn's pink lips, murmuring an oath of loathing. Luckily, King Arthur was found afloat on a boat in his moat, and Tolivar did, with a mighty blow, cut his manhood off smartly.

"Twitch, you son-of-a-bitch," Tolivar said, "your law was without foundation. Such unfair commands brings confusion to all your inhabitants waiting in wordsmith prison spinning odious circumlocutions. Grammar and word construction must grow as folks would wish. I shall allow man and woman to talk without prior conditions or limitations. Still, folks must maintain strict rituals and thus I will prohibit milk and animals touching. I claim your land, your grammar, your food laws and Lady Gwynn who by my sword, will not mount a pig again."

Tolivar and Gwynn did join in conjugal bliss, without inhibitions, cohabiting mirthfully for many moons. And Tolivar did not oink at all, for his body was in fantastic condition. Lady Gywnn gladly saw that without garb, his manhood stood up smartly. Our Lady, an unusually shy woman did, upon this and various occasions, cry out odious idioms, an indication of Gwynn's unusually high physical satisfaction. And from that day on, lunch was always *milchig*.

❑

Note: Although possibly apocryphal, this lost tract of Rabbi Nachman Brachman is proof of anti-pig goings on by Knights of Judaic pursuasion at King Arthur's court, and, as such, lays the foundation for the laws of *Kashrut*.

Flour and Salt

EVA MARCUS WATCHED BONGO MAN EATING GIANT HELICOPTERS made out of green plastic because that was her eight year old brother Aron's favorite TV program. Eva knew that the helicopter was just a toy, and Bongo Man was only an actor in costume and make up, and she was tired of all that.

Aron switched the channel to a cartoon about a little boy who had magical powers to change himself into all kinds of animals, but she knew they were only pictures that someone had drawn and not real. Eleven-year-olds are very good at knowing the difference between real and fake.

Eva stuck out her tongue at her brother who had done nothing to deserve it and stamped her foot. "TV is fake! There's nothing going on. I want something to do!"

"Shh," said her mother who had just come home from work and had a headache, "you're making too much noise."

"Shut up," said Eva's brother. "Or I'll kick you in the head."

"I am tired of everything," said Eva to herself. "Tired of watching fake things on TV, tired of doing homework, tired of helping around the house." She wanted something to do. She asked friends to play, but they were all watching TV or playing computer games. Eva didn't want fake electronic friends, she wanted a real friend to play with.

"Did you do your Hebrew homework?" asked mother when Eva complained she had nothing to do and no one to be with.

"Not all of it." Eva was twelve years old and learning the Hebrew *aleph-bet*, which was part of her Bat Mitzvah training.

"Who wants to read Hebrew, anyway?" cried Eva. "You can't talk to anybody with it.

"Except God," said her brother, "And people in Israel, and kids who go to Hebrew school." Aron acted like he knew everything.

"It's just another stupid waste of time," said Eva"Nobody listens to me in English, why should I learn Hebrew?"

"Instead of watching TV, you better study," Mom warned. "Your teacher wants you to learn the *aleph-bet* by Tuesday."

So Eva turned to her toys. She had talking interactive computer games and all kinds of battery powered robots, cars that bumped into furniture, dolls that spoke pre-recorded messages, or even repeated whatever she said on a hidden tape recorder. She pressed the button of Aron's electric train set and with a blank stare, watched the cars race around on their tracks.

Eva just wanted something fun to do as she decided to work with dough like her mother made from flour, water and salt. Real clay was dirty and too mess.

"Well, flour comes from wheat, and wheat comes from the earth," said her mother. "So, really, it's like clay."

"And salt," said Aron, "comes from oceans of tears."

But Eva knew, that no matter what anyone said about it, there was a difference between dough and clay. As she worked with the dough, she began to feel a little better because she could make things; a snake, and a ball, even people. Then she could squash them all and put them back into the ball they came from.

It was on this day that Eva decided to make a playmate for herself by using the kind of magical powers Bongo Man had. Her new friend wouldn't be a superhero or a Frankenstein monster. She would just be a good and kind companion.

Her Hebrew teacher had told the class about the Vilna Goan who had made a *golem* before he was even thirteen years old, and Rabbi Lowe of Prague who had made a *golem* from clay a long time ago. Eva saw no reason why she couldn't do the same. The difference would be that she would make a girl creature who would be much, much nicer than any of the *golems* made by men in the image of themselves. She would make her *golem* in the image of herself, and she would call her "Lem" for short.

So Eva went into the kitchen when her mother wasn't around, and mixed up a batch of flour and water and salt, and added a few of her own tears. She recited an incantation which consisted of reading all the letters of the Hebrew alphabet forward as well as backwards. Then she marched around the bowl of dough three times.

At first Eva's figurine was just a ball of play dough with two feet, but the more she worked, the more human the sculpture looked. Lem was a short figure with thin legs and four tiny fingers on each hand. In the back of her head was a special battery compartment, and there was a little depression in her mouth, where a tiny piece of paper might be put. The *golem* looked quite pale, hair and eyes and skin all the same pasty white color; but she looked friendly and harmless. Eva rolled some short, flat pieces of dough for hair, and as a finishing touch, made a heart out of a bit of extra dough.

When mother called for dinner, Eva didn't want to come down from her room until after she had finished her project. When it was done and no one was in the kitchen, Eva baked her creature in the microwave oven. After baking, Lem was a light golden tan, with no belly button, of course, and her large friendly heart secured to her body with Eva's tears. Eva hid Lem in her room in a dark toy chest so the *golem* could cool down.

As soon as she came home from school the next day, Eva did her Hebrew homework, and practiced writing the entire *aleph-bet*. And because she was ecologically minded, she wrote on both sides of the paper. She wrote the letters out of order, up and down, forwards and backwards just for fun, and made up all kinds of words; some that didn't even exist, and although she didn't know it, by chance one of the words was the secret name for God. She knew the Vilna Goan had written the word *emes* (truth) on his *golem's* head, figuring that should he need to stop the *golem,* he could take off the "e" and then the word would mean "end." And that would be the end of the *golem.* Rather than write on Lem's head, Eva had written the word "friend" on an old T-shirt for the *golem* to waer. And if the *golem* became too big for her breaches, Eva would scratch out the "Fri" and only "end" would be left. And that would be the "end" of Lem.

Now, unbeknown to even the wisest, most learned grown-ups, all babies at birth know the secret name of God and that is why they learn more things in a day than any adult could in a year. Because the power of this name is so great, just saying it or writing it conjures wonders even if you don't necessarily know you've said or written the hidden name. By the time infants can pronounce it, they forget it. And the reason they no longer remember is simple. If everyone knew the name, it wouldn't be a secret anymore. And if it wasn't a secret, some of the names inherent potency might be captured by evil forces.

Eva decided to put the letter *aleph*—the one letter that all other Hebrew letters are supposed to be derived from—in the dough-creature's mouth so that she could learn Hebrew. By chance, Eva wrote an *aleph* on the back of the paper with the secret word for God on it. The combination of God's real name and the letter *aleph* gave her creature the ability to talk and think.

Eva took two old C-batteries from the train set to energize her newly made creature, never dreaming that the *golem* was brought to life by quite another power.

Eva went to bed happy that night, had a good time in school the next day because she had practiced so hard at home making her letters perfect. One day, the little girl had the bright idea of asking Lem to help her with her assignments and from that time on, Lem did all the Hebrew home work and everything else that was asked of her, with ease.

The *golem* was a charming, cooperative, pleasant new companion who did everything Eva wanted, which made it easy for Eva to give her power to learn and grow to the *golem*. It was not that the *golem* was bad. The *golem*, for her part, seemed to be pleased to wear the T-shirt for she knew nothing of clothes. The *golem*, when she was made, did not ask to be made, and did not ask to be anything but herself. But, the more human she became, the more she began to have a mind of her own.

When Eva came home one day, her little brother Aron was watching re-runs of Bugs Bunny cartoons which he loved, because no matter how many times Bugs got caught by Elmer, fell down a cliff, got blown up or run over, he always got right up again, unharmed.

That night at bedtime, while her mother and father were watching a TV show about a happy family of three going on vacation to California, Eva was getting ready for bed when suddenly Lem spoke. She was not all that surprised about Lem talking; Eva just thought that the battery must be working, but she never suspected that quite another force had taken over.

At first, the new creature, with its softly awkward body, was more stupid than Eva's simplest robot. Lem asked no questions because there were no thoughts in her head that Eva hadn't put there. Lem did everything that Eva asked.

Since Eva decided not to tell her parents about her wonderful new toy, there was nothing Lem could do outside of Eva's room. So Eva continued to have Lem do all her homework, clean her room and lay out her clothes for school. One of the rules of *golemhood* is that they must serve their human masters, and do anything that was asked.

The funny toy grew smarter every day. She learned Hebrew and English at the same time and repeated everything Eva said, just like a tape recorder, and gradually began to make sentences of her own. Often Lem just babbled *aleph-bet* sounds to herself, and just like a real baby, babbled the secret name of God, which gave the *golem* much more power than she had before.

Lem wore the old outgrown T-shirt with the word friend lettered on it and lived contentedly in the large toy chest when she wasn't busy doing homework or chores. Eva saw that the creature was brighter than she had first suspected, so she gave the *golem* her spelling and history assignments too. Lem began to learn about the nature of the world in which she was living.

All went well for a while. Every Shabbat, Eva took the magic paper out of Lem's mouth, for *golemkind* as well as mankind, ought to have a day of rest.

❏

As time went by, the *golem* grew from the size of a small baby doll to the size of Eva herself. Every evening when the rest of the family watched television, Eva went to her room. She got into the habit of never even bothering to read her school books or check how well the *golem* was doing the homework, because the *golem* always did everything right the first time. Soon Lem spoke perfect Hebrew as well as English and got A's on all the report cards. In truth, the *golem* had become smarter than her master.

In the meantime, Eva began to know less and less about the world; her reading suffered, her language skills did not develop and she could not keep up with the other children. She didn't worry about it, for as long as the *golem* did all the homework, Eva could pass Lem's work off as her's. Yet she knew in the deep recesses of her heart, that as the *golem* grew more and more human, she was becoming more and more ignorant.

One Friday afternoon, when Eva's mother had finished setting up everything for Shabbat dinner and was taking a break to watch a program showing how a happy family of four could build a swimming pool together, she asked Eva to bike over to the kosher bakery to pick up a *challah*. Eva left Lem in her room, and asked her to put away her toys and lay out her Sabbath dress.

Phoebe Frank
© 1996

This time, when Lem saw the dress—dark velvet trimmed with real lace on the collar—jealousy began to grow in her doughy heart, and because she was not human, Lem did not question herself about any of her feelings. She simply wanted to wear the lovely dress and since she had never been told its unseemly for a golem to want to be beautiful, she did not know she was doing anything wrong. Lem slipped off the T-shirt with the word "Friend" on it that she always wore, and struggled to put on the dress. As the sun began to sink, the *golem* thought her own thoughts, which was not exactly in the *golem* rules. When Eva returned with the *challah*, she found Lem sitting dejectedly on the side of her bed, half in and half out of her dress.

"You must never do that again," cried Eva. "You are just a *golem*, not a human, and wearing such a beautiful dress would be ridiculous." The *golem* said not a word, but because the *aleph* and the secret name of God were in her head, she continued to think her own thoughts.

"Here," said Eva, "Put your T-shirt back on, and be my friend again." The *golem* wasn't too happy about this, but did as she was told.

❑

Eva's mother made a wonderful roast chicken for Shabbat and her father brought flowers. After dinner they all rushed off to services and Eva forgot to take the paper out of the *golem's* mouth and the batteries out of their special compartment as she usually did on Shabbat.

While the family was at synagogue, the *golem* experienced more urgent desires to be human. She began to grow larger, to use the words in her mouth in new and dangerous ways. She got so big she split all the seams in the "Friend" T-shirt. She did not want to be a friend any longer. She roamed through Eva's closet pulling out one after another of her best dresses until she found the dress with the real lace collar and she struggled to put it on. The seams were very tight because her arms were so big, but the golem, in her frenzy, didn't notice. The ungainly creature ran to Eva's mother's room to paint herself with eye makeup and lipstick and knocked over and spilled her cosmetics on the bathroom counter. The golem thought herself beautiful, but her face was a strange whitish gray color, like the underbelly of a fish. Her eyes were ringed with turquoise eye shadow and her lips were the color of blood. Satisfied with herself, the golem smashed and crashed through the dining room, living room, and then finally out the front door and ran to the synagogue to sit with the family like a real person.

❑

The golem entered the synagogue riding a great rush of wind. The congregants felt suddenly chilled and stared at the strange creature who roared up and down the aisles looking for Eva. Eva sat with her family and as they looked up from their prayer books, they suddenly discovered a terrible creature trying to wedge herself in the pew with them. Eva looked at Lem, brightly painted with her mothers make-up, and suddenly Eva realized that she had not deactivated Lem.

There was the golem, bigger than Eva herself, wearing the beautiful Sabbath dress over her clumsy body, racing about like a mad dog, chattering and jabbering to herself. Her face was as lumpy as a baroque pearl and her madly glowing eyes were ringed with turquoise shadow.

Eva felt helpless. She did not know Hebrew well enough to command the *golem* to stop, and English was no help at all. Then she realized she did not know anything. It was the *golem*, not Eva, who had studied the Torah, and the writings of the prophets in preparation for the Bat Mitzvah. It was the *golem* who had studied Hebrew and history and the *golem* who had the secret name of God in her head, not Eva. And it was now Eva, who felt like a lifeless, stupid ball of clay.

All she could do was to watch in horror as the *golem* drew fiery currents of electricity from the air herself. As Lem laughed and danced and sang snippets of prayers in front of the terrified congregation, Eva could see the paper in the *golem's* mouth. She had to do something and fast.

"Lem! Tie my shoes!" she commanded in her sternest voice. Since the *golem's* chief purpose in life was to obey, she suspended her frenzy in mid-air to bow at Eva's feet. Eva stuck her finger in the *golem's* mouth and ripped out the magical paper. And quite a spectacle it was. The *golem* hung for a moment motionless in mid-air. Her strange contorted face puffed up with rouged cheeks, and her mad eyes saw in that instant that her destiny was to be just what she had always been; a combination of flour and salt mixed with water. And that of course, in a certain way, is how it is with human beings. They are destined to be just what they are. When the *golem* realized that there was no more magic holding her together, she collapsed lifelessly at Eva's feet. The battery door flew open, and the C-batteries fell out and rolled in the aisle. Eva's lovely dress disintegrated, and all that was left of the *golem* was the T-shirt she had worn under the dress, and all that could be seen of that was the word "end," crumpled on the floor, covering a small ball of dough.

Her parents and brother rushed to Eva's side. Aron thought it the best trick he had ever seen, but her parents faces, along with the other congregants, were white with fear. The rabbi took control of his senses and called on *Elohaynu* to protect them all; the cantor and choir ended services with a rapid rendition of *Adon Olam,* and they all streamed out of the temple as fast as possible. After it was all over, Eva's family wondered if they had ever seen anything like that on TV, and they had to admit they had not.

Eva picked up the pitiful ball of dough. All Lem's knowledge had gone into the wind, not into Eva. Eva took what was left of the dough home as a reminder of how she had almost traded knowledge of the world for a *golem,* who was after all, nothing but flour, water, and salt. And salt, as her brother could tell you, is made from oceans of tears. ❑

Recipe for a *Golem*

Flour	as needed	**Salt**	a touch
Tears	to soften	**Incantation**	whatever works

Small Piece of Parchment or Paper. Write every combination of Hebrew letters on the paper in order to find the secret Name of God. Roll up the paper.

Mix all ingredients until palpable. Form as desired. Before baking, roll a small part of the dough into a heart using a knife. With the end of a spoon make a small cavity in the *golem's* mouth and a battery compartment at the back of its head. Secure heart onto body using tears to glue in place. Bake on a well greased flat pan in a hot-as-hell oven until a light golden color and cheeks puff. When cooled, insert paper with secret name of God into *golem's* mouth.

Allow *golem* to rest until cool. Keep out of sight in a dark place. Use sparingly. **Serves one.**

Fifty Steps

WE TAKE NUMBERS, INCHING FORWARD, waiting to see the high priests in white jackets, aprons and chef's hats made of white paper. Under the puffed hat that sits like an old hen on a bald nest, lies the *yarmulke,* little black skull cap. Rosettes of blood on the aprons. You have to expect that in a butcher shop. It feels like a hospital, something sacred and clandestine.

Those butchers are always so sly. "You want a piece of meat?" and they laugh a little, so it means, "Do you want to do it?" The green walls bring out the red color of the meat and the butcher's passion isn't necessarily brisket.

Don't think I don't know about these butchers, how they flirt. I've been buying meat here for years, and I know what they're saying when they tell you the pot roast looks good. These days you're lucky to get one who speaks English. Behind the counter the butchers are all Israeli or Spanish or Chinese. They are watched by a watcher, the *Mashgiach,* especially trained to make sure everything is done right. That's a Jew who knows the intricate rituals of keeping kosher.

The butchers don't have to be Jewish once the meat is dead, but to slaughter animals, that's a horse of a different cut. Ritual slaughterers must be Jewish, are often unemployed rabbis and have special training. They make sure the animal doesn't suffer, that the knife is sharp and without defect. Things like that. No one makes sure that people don't suffer, though.

"How you doing?" says Manny, or Sammy Wong or Roberto. They have these long knives sharp enough to cut through trees.

"Trim it," I say. "No fat."

Roberto smiles in a way that says I'll show you how to cook brisket, I'll show what you want to know. These same guys sell coleslaw and dill pickles, blood speckles on their hands even after they've washed. You can never get all the blood off.

They smile over the dead turkeys and chickens robbed of pin feathers.

"You want a leg of lamb, a breast?" Who couldn't catch their meaning over the lamb chops, smugly in rows, over the flanken, skirt steak, fillets, hamburger meat and eye of round? I skip the lamb, it's too expensive. Nice with mint jelly.

The butchers always smile because they are selling me ten times more than I need or want. I don't know how many ounces I need per person, or how long to cook the turkey at three hundred fifty degrees, how to divide pounds by hours.

They teach me to cook. "Broil it, a little salt and pepper. What could be bad? Maybe I'll come taste it," Sammy Wong says, eyes black as peppercorns, suggesting black things. I hate when I get him. I try to stand in back and let someone else take my number, but he always sees me and he says, "Hi! Mrs. Roth, how you doing?" I know what he wants to taste. He probably tasted the previous Mrs. Roth, Selma. She also shops here. They know everything, these butchers.

All that red meat, so waxy, could these ribs and shoulders ever have been alive? Walking around on feet?

My grandfather was a butcher, sawdust on the floor. He was a kosher butcher and didn't have to work Saturdays. The family secret was that on Saturdays, he sold cars.

I just came home. All the packages are wrapped in paper white as fat, each a sacred bundle soon to taste the ice in my freezer. Tomorrow is Rosh HaShonah, and my husband's mother is coming to dinner along with my folks and all the grandchildren, and a few friends. My husband's mother liked Selma better than me.

Shopping is the first step in making the holiday meal. I would rather be out robbing banks. I don't actually know how to rob a bank, but it's less bother than cooking. Each step gets harder. I load the car, step two. The car is filled with bags. The car is my armor, I bet I could rob banks and get away with it, but my basic training is in shopping. Unload the groceries, step three. I get tired carrying. This September day is in the nineties in Los Angeles. Now the kitchen is full of bags. You think I'm complaining? Sure, there are people who have no groceries, have no money, have no cars.

"What are you complaining about? You have it easy." My husband says this to me when I talk to him in his car on the car phone. "Pity the homeless," he says. "You're always dissatisfied. Be grateful for what you have."

I am not sufficiently grateful.

"What do you want?" he asks, but doesn't listen when I tell him.

There are rules. Feel the tomatoes, knock the melons, haggle with the pot roast, cut out the fat. You are supposed to care about these things.

I'm doing step four, putting away. When my husband is home we watch television. We only talk when he's in the car, when we can't see each other. We talk because he's bored driving. He puts in long hours as a computer salesman, and he calls when I'm not listening or wanting to listen like now when I'm putting away. I am planning dinner, step five. I suppose step one should be to write the menu so you know what to buy. I usually buy and then try to use what I have.

My husband sits down in front of the refrigerator once a week and goes through the old foods, something unidentifiable in a plastic crypt. "Why did you buy this? Why that?"

I have no answers.

Step six is hunting for the right size dishes and pots and pans. Seven is chopping, stirring, baking, mixing. Eight, cleaning the kitchen before the company comes, so it should look nice and shiny like you didn't work in it at all. Nine is serving. Of course you can't sit down with your guests. I hate the ones who say, "We can't eat until you do." Don't come to my house, I want to say, because if those are the conditions, you'll never eat. I skate around the table waiting on them. They manage to eat all right.

I'm too tired to talk. I can't be witty when I'm worried about things like overcooking the rice, unmolding the Jell-O. Who will spill? What will break? What will I forget? I'm on automatic. If I drink wine, I'll fall asleep on my plate.

The fiftieth step is putting away the dishes. I'm skipping a lot of steps in between finishing the meal and going to bed.

My husband likes to tell me certain wonderful things about his ex. I told him I don't like to hear good things about Selma. Only tell me the dirt, all the bad stuff about the ex. How she is a knockkneed shrew. I like that kind of thing. If you have to tell something good, which you shouldn't, it should be in a category that doesn't matter. Like how the ex was good at changing tires or making meat loaf. Two categories not worth competing in.

The next holiday, Yom Kippur, is coming soon. Back to the butcher. This time maybe I'll try lamb chops. My husband said Selma never bought lamb chops. She is a blonde, of course dyed. Not a very flattering color on her. They were married, lived in Encino. After the split he got the couches, she got the stereo. She got the Caddie, he the Honda. I got her husband—and the butcher.

❑

A Good Name

SHORTLY BEFORE I WAS BORN IN 1934, I had a run-in with Ferdy the name broker in Heaven. His name was meant to be "Freddy," but in the days before we had a name broker to assist with selection or check clerical errors, that kind of thing often happened. The Chief Counselor needed administrative help and Ferdy was chosen, not so much for his empathy, but for his determination to go by the rules.

Ferdy, wearing mirrored sunglasses, sat at a huge transparent desk shuffling papers. He had military hair and loosely connected teeth.

The nearest I can come to describing Heaven's Name Bank is that it was like being inside an enormous hologram. When you entered the cavernous room, you could barely make out that a man was seated there, working a computer — and when you reached out to touch anything, there were only colored lights shining on your hand. This is the place you come to choose a name just before you're born and you don't have a lot of time to think about it.

The brightness of the place was blinding after the dark womb of my development. When Ferdy leaned forward and asked for my name application, I could see myself reflected in his lenses. I wasn't a pretty sight, but I had potential.

I was at the Name Bank to make my selection because a good name is like a good dog. If you treat it respectfully, it will follow you the rest of your life, but, if you kick it, it might just turn around and bite you.

Ferdy touched a button and the light in the room became softer and more respectful. "What kind of name do you want?"

I asked for one that would become famous.

"Famous makes it harder," he said. "More forms, more bureaucracy. You'll first have to specify choice of religion and gender."

"Jewish and female would be nice."

"Well, that's OK, we have plenty of requests for Jewish baby girls." Ferdy and the room glowed as though they were one entity. "Did you have something in mind?"

"I was thinking of Moses."

"Moses? What are you, crazy? You said you wanted to be a Jewish woman. That's a man's name. There isn't a female counterpart to Moses. Even if you were a man, you couldn't get Moses." Suddenly the room was pulsating with intense color, as though I had said the wrong thing.

"Why can't I be Moses?" I asked.

"You lack humility. Even Moses didn't want to be Moses."

I didn't like his attitude. He began to tap his finger on the desk and glowed brightly. He was in a hurry to finish.

"Men and women have different kinds of names? Is that standard practice?" I asked.

"Worldwide. And they lead different kinds of lives."

Though his eyes were hidden behind the glasses, I could feel him staring at me.

"You could be Danielle Aarons. You'd be President of Hadassah, write five major cookbooks and marry a doctor who sits at the Western Wall. It's a nice life, it suits your needs."

I got angry. "I don't want to get respect just because I married well. And I don't want a down-sized man's name. I want to be a Jewish woman who is famous. Could we get on with it?"

Ferdy purpled. "Let me be sure I understand you. You say you don't want male, even though there are definite advantages. For example, if you were a man you could be political — a famous Menachem. Or we could put you into something artistic or scientific. For example, if you wanted to be Eli Mendleson, we could put you in an executive suite with two secretaries. You'd have a lifetime cholesterol under two hundred, and accidental death while water skiing at age eighty. A beautiful life. Yours for the asking."

"No, thanks. My mind is made up."

"All right," said Ferdy. "It's a go on the gender thing. Don't say I didn't warn you. But are you sure you want Jewish? Wouldn't you like something a little less — stressful? We have vacancies in the Baptist section. Nice water rituals."

"Thanks, but I'll stick with my choices."

"But why Jewish?" The room vibrated with colored lights. "That's not one of our more popular groups."

Ferdy tapped a finger on the desk, making a tiny pinging sound. I wondered if all the name brokers were like him. With that kind of attitude I could see why Judaism wasn't sold out.

"I didn't think I was cut out to be a Suarez or an O'Toole," I said. Jewish seemed a good choice; you got a lot of holidays and what you did in your head was your own business.

The computer had two television screens that blinked like eyes, and a large slit beneath each that looked like a mouth. The name broker inserted my applicationto be born as a Jewish girl in the slot and it disappeared. The machine gurgled and gulped and sighed some interior sorrow. In a few moments the paper came back with a large gold "accepted" stamped on it.

Ferdy's face was stern as he reviewed the application. A tap on a key and information danced across the screen. All the while we spoke, the broker watched the tube intently, finally looking up. "We've got to get going on the name. It's almost time for you to be born. Do you have any other ideas?"

I looked at my list, written on a small compressed, opaque cloud. I had heard the Bank was running low on names. I was afraid they'd have only irregulars left, or some off-brand stuff that had been picked over. I didn't want generics. I wanted top-of-the-line brand names. I took the plunge. "Barbara Walters?"

"Taken — two years ago."

"Shana Alexander?"

"I don't know," he said. "It has a bitchy sound to it."

"Elizabeth Taylor?"

"Just as bad and out of the question. If you wanted converted you should have specified before. What else?"

Famous seemed to be slipping away. "I'd like something glitzy, something with silver sparkles like the ones in your display." The names in the Name Bank window were elegant and thin; Christine Johnson, Diana Livingston; size six personas that could wear tight skirts and minimal lingerie. They would marry Paul Caldwell and Harrison Waverly, drive Ferraris and live in Bel Aire.

Ferdy looked me over. "If you only had been earlier, I could have given you Lana Smythe-Finkelstein. She got her name half-price. She'll have twins when she's thirty, drive car pools until forty, leave Smythe in her fifties, and when she's sixty, her new husband (Mr. Finkelstein) will gift her with a matched pair of treadmill tests at the Mayo Clinic. It doesn't get much better than that."

I said nothing.

Ferdy tried a different approach. "Look at me, I'm not famous and I've been happily employed for eons."

So what? I thought. I was beginning to see what men were like.

Ferdy's forehead pulsed with agitation. The lights in the room went psychedelic. "Don't worry so much about being famous. Why don't you just go for a name that fits? And if it's too big or too small, we'll alter it for free. Maybe you could update an old standard."

"No, thanks," I repeated. Those traditional names were pretty shopworn. I consulted my list of dwindling possibilities. "Ling May Schwartz has a nice ring."

"Your mother wouldn't stop crying."

"Don't you have any opportunities for someone like me?"

Ferdy pressed a key and a new screen flashed into view. He skimmed the message.

"Yes, the Mandlebaums from Chicago just this minute applied for a girl. That's the slot you'll fill. The only choice you have now is your given name, do that and you're on your way."

"Have my parents-to-be sent in any name requests?"

"She's been reading name books, your Mom. She likes Greek mythology."

"But I'd rather have Missy, Darla or Tina." Tina. That would be a great name, I would grow up to wear beige and small buttons. I would have California blonde hair and a nose job when I was sixteen.

Ferdy sighed in annoyance. Name brokers didn't like you taking so long to decide. The intensity of the light had lessened considerably. He suggested Bracha, Ziva and Shoshanna. "What about Zona? You might make some money with it."

"Isn't that the Hebrew word for hooker? I thought you were supposed to make good suggestions."

"A slight misinterpretation of our policy. I'm supposed to be helpful. Goodness is discretionary."

A photograph materialized in front of me.

"Zona," he pointed out, "Comes with a gold bracelet with the name spelled out in diamonds. That name is on our incentive plan." He was trying to hurry me along.

"Out of the question," I shrugged. Ferdy said I had to make up my mind immediately because the birth canal was opening.

"I can see you're a hardship case, so tell you what I'm going to do." He walked over to a filing cabinet and pulled out an old diskette. "I haven't put these back into the system yet. They're leftovers from our recycling and reincarnation program."

He displayed a frayed group of names on the screen before me. He pointed to the "P" section. "How about Phoebus? It's a bit on the unusual side, and your mom wants Greek. It's perfect."

"That doesn't sound like a girl's name," I said suspiciously.

Ferdy smiled as though there was something stuck between his teeth. "Well, you're right about that," he said, "but we can send it to our alteration department and have it down-sized to fit you. It's a great name. Comes from Phoebus Apollo, the sun god. Means bright and shining. Not a bad neighborhood to be from, right? Dont worry about a thing, we can design it to suit your individual needs, make it, ah, more feminine. Shorten it a little. Just watch the screen."

He pushed a button, typed in the name and the monitor displayed a huge room of elderly tailors bending over sewing machines. Each had a box of names on his work table. "You'll see. We'll make it fit. No extra charge."

"Wait a minute. A tailor's sweat shop in heaven? That doesn't seem right."

"We prefer to think of it as our Customer Service Department." He was offended. "Anyway, angels don't sweat. Dewy, maybe, from upper atmospheric conditions."

"Phoebus? It's too hard to spell," I cried. "It's not phonetic. No, no. That's not me. I don't care how many tailors you have designing it!"

"Have patience, please. Your name is being processed." Ferdy spoke to the computer screen. "Morris. Get that Phoebus name up here, ASAP and change it to Phoebe, as a favor to the little lady."

Finally an elderly man appeared on the screen holding up a newly stitched name. "Phoebe," it said.

"What? What kind of name is Phoebe? It's too fat. If I had 'Phoebe' I'd be a spinster, have hairy arms, walk with a limp and retire from a nursing career with gout. Give me something like Desiree, Esmee or Astrid."

"What nonsense. Fitting names is a lost art. Morris is one of the best," he said. "This Phoebe will be fair, marry a Yecke and have three great kids. Phoebe is a name they'll remember. It's a name that will stick to you. You'll never lose it. It fits you "

On the television screen in front of Ferdy, I saw a flash of my birth tunnel opening up. My body felt lighter as I floated effortlessly toward the tube. I was about to enter it and be born.

"Oh, God. I'm not ready. How about Star Dancer?" Yes, Star Dancer was definitely me. I could see that name in lights. It had charisma, charm.

"Too Indian. Definitely out of the question," said Ferdy.

I was desperate. "Golda Meier? Rosanne Barr?"

Jagged bolts of lightning flashed across the room. The screen steamed white with rage; they don't have much of a sense of humor up there. The birth canal continued to open and I was suddenly propelled toward it.

"I'm afraid you don't have any more time to consider this matter. You'll have to take Phoebe," and he handed me a tiny bracelet with the name Phoebe Mandlebaum printed on the beads. "We'll send our Counselor down to tell your folks your name."

"Phoebe doesn't feel famous at all," I sobbed. "It's not me, take it back to the sweat shop."

Ferdy leaned towards me and pushed me into the television set feet first. "My dear young lady, you just don't seem to understand. Your name doesn't make you, you make your name."

With that, I was sucked bodily into the tunnel, wearing my beaded bracelet, but still hoping that by some miracle I would turn out to be Rosanne. I would be famous and at least I could eat.

The experience of being born wasn't so bad; it was like going down a water chute and there was somebody dressed in green to catch me.

The Counselor had already arrived in the room and was whispering my name into my mother's ear. Mom smiled. "Thank you, she said. "I always wanted a name for our daughter that meant *bright and shining*."

A woman in white washed me off and brought me to my mom who counted my toes and fingers. "Welcome, baby Phoebe," my folks cooed.

And so I'm Phoebe, a name that has stuck to me, a name that fits. After all, it was tailor made.

❏

The Right Man for the Job

WHEN THE DARK-HAIRED YOUNG MAN, RABBI ARI KREMER, tried to button his old gabardine raincoat, the button fell off in his hand. He put it in his pocket and continued to walk with his head down against the sleeting rain, carefully picking his way through the puddles on Fairfax Avenue. His old blue T-shirt and baggy slacks felt damp. His feet were wet; the thin soles of his well-worn shoes sucked the water up from the pavement, making his socks adhere to his skin.

The Fairfax District, one of the last remaining outposts of Jewish street life in Los Angeles, was still waking up to the peculiar smell of freshly baked bread, singed cooking oil and bus fumes. The old ladies had not yet appeared with their two-wheeled grocery carts, the *schwarma* (roasted meat on a spit) and *falafel* (fried balls of chickpeas) stands had just opened up.

Kremer passed Neustedder's shoe store, with its rich display of oxfords, running shoes and leather boots. He knew Aaron Neustedder would give him a good deal, but figured that if he made do with his old loafers, he could buy a copy of the biblical concordance at Sojcer's bookstore. He was anxious to impress the congregants in his new (and first) post as a rabbi at Beth Ha Or Synagogue.

The concordance, a text he'd had his eye on ever since seminary days, would help him to achieve the brilliance, and perhaps the confidence, he hungered for. This masterful directory of Hebrew words and phrases in the first Five Books of Moses, could give a scholarly and elegant gloss to his sermons.

Although he worked, reworked and overworked his speeches, he could not find a way to touch his congregants. As they listened to him with vacant faces, he imagined they dreamed only of getting a fast mini-Danish and a cup of coffee at the *Oneg Shabbat* (refreshments following the Sabbath service) before they drove home.

When the congregants shook his hand on the way out and politely praised his speech, he looked into their eyes to see if he had kindled any sparks, but they were looking in the direction of the social hall, where the sweets were waiting.

In addition to the concordance, he had been asked to buy a Torah for his new congregation. He had never bought a Torah before, and while he was elated by his assignment, he couldn't understand why the interviewing committee had hired him in the first place. Didn't they mind his high-pitched voice? Notice his prominent Adam's Apple that bobbed wildly when he was nervous? Couldn't they see how unsure he was of himself?

Leading services was not a problem, selecting the prayers, making announcements—none of these bothered him. But the sermon was a different story. He remembered his old teacher, Rabbi Emil Horner, saying there was only one sermon he could ever give anyway. Be a *mensch* and a good Jew. Everything else was commentary.

While the advice was good, it didn't tell him how to reach into his congregants' hearts. Whenever he addressed the membership, he could feel his knees shake, the insides of his stomach turn somersaults. He was a fish out of water, gulping for air.

He desperately wanted to speak without notes, but he used them because he was afraid he would not remember the important points. Using an outline or index cards made him fear he would lose his place and stutter. So he plodded on, word for word, reading the entire sermon in a monotone. When he faltered, as he usually did, he would go red with shame, barely holding himself together as his voice became higher and higher. He would race toward his ending like a riderless horse heading for the corral, free of burden.

His father had helped him in school, used to correct his papers, retype his outlines, correct his English. Then, when Ari decided on rabbinical training at the University of Judaism in Los Angeles, suddenly there was no one to do the homework but himself.

He feared he could never live up to his father's expectations. His father loved him, but looked on his son as a well-meaning boob. Who makes a living as a professional Jew?

"A man with your brains," said his father, "could be anything. A doctor, a lawyer, a businessman. How will you raise a family, what kind of job is this for a nice Jewish boy?"

Ari tried to stammer out that he liked Jewish history, as well as the idea of "helping people." He loved immersing himself in the Talmud, the study and discipline of it. Besides, he thought to himself, Jewish studies was the one area his father knew nothing about. The elder Kremer considered the Bible useful enough for holding up the short leg of a table and nothing more.

Ari sighed as he approached his destination. The fact that he knew he wasn't the congregation's first choice added to his insecurities. He was not a commanding figure like the rabbi from Detroit, Rabbi Eli Sossner. The five-foot-six Ari Kremer was barrel-chested, and stocky. No matter how often he shaved, he always looked like he needed one. When Ari conducted services, Murray Gendleman, the men's club president, discreetly placed a small stepping stool behind the lectern for him to stand upon.

Rabbi Sossner, unlike Ari, had the reputation for giving inspiring sermons. He could coin a phrase as easily as most people turn the corner, and embroider a theme like a seamstress with a golden needle. But the dignified gentleman had taken one look at the facilities the new congregation rented from the Elk's lodge and turned around as rapidly as his shiny Ferregamo shoes could take him.

Perhaps the selection committee was simply demoralized after Sossner turned them down and chose Kremer despite his protestations to Gendleman that he might not be the right man for the job. It was a brand new congregation and the right man would be the key to attracting members.

A week after being hired, Gendleman asked Ari to purchase the first Torah for the ark.

Ari's Adam's apple bobbed up and down when he asked Gendleman to come with him to Sojcer's Judaica shop, but Gendleman had to work. The president advised him that the only thing he had to remember was to stay within the board's budget. "We are not rich, so just get a good deal," he said, "and we'll be happy." The rabbi invited Murray's wife, the president of the sisterhood, but she was going to a Hadassah luncheon. He asked his own wife, Dahlia, but she had to drive the nursery school car pool. Both ways.

So it was that he set out alone, the congregation's checkbook in one hand and his personal funds for the concordance in the other. He felt like Jack in the fairy tale about a boy who bought beans instead of a good cow. Ari desperately wanted to avoid making a mistake. He wanted to end up with the golden egg.

He entered the shop a few minutes after Max Sperling opened for business and the shopkeeper set out a few Torah scrolls on the back counter for the young Rabbi to inspect. Ari liked Max. Over six feet tall, with an unruly white beard, Max looked more like a rabbi than Ari.

The store was long and narrow with locked shelves filled with gleaming silver ritual objects; spice boxes, candlesticks, water pitchers, *challah* knives, Pesach plates, three-tiered matzah holders. Max placed two pristine Torah scrolls on the counter, both completed last year; one from Williamsburg, New York, and the other made in Israel. Both of them had well- spaced, even characters written with rich black ink that stood out clearly on the perfect white parchment. These Torahs were unused, thought Ari, just like himself. The modern scrolls were much more costly than the third Torah Sperling laid on the counter. This one had been completed around the turn of the century. Its vellum was a uniform, deep gold color, and the text was written with a fine, even hand.

Every *Sefer Torah*, from the very earliest to the most modern, was identical with respect to the text and the placement of the words on each section or *chelek*. The other variables were the age and condition of the scroll, and the type of wood used in the rollers, the *etz hayim*.

Ari's face fell. The beautiful new Torahs cost many times more than his budget allowed.

"What kind of a Torah did you want?" asked Max as Ari picked up the heavy old scroll. It was still more than he could afford.

"Well, uhm, I thought it would be a good idea to get one with light weight *etz hayim*, so it would be easier for the old people to lift up and dance with on *Simchas Torah*." This ritual celebration commemorating the giving of the Torah meant a lot to Ari. He wanted everyone in the congregation to have the experience of actually having been at Sinai when the Torah was handed down.

Sperling looked up for just a moment and narrowed his eyes.

Ari thought he probably sounded like a fool just then. He should have had a loftier set of criterion in mind. He should have spoken of desiring excellence in the way the scribe calligraphed the letters, crowns and adornments.

Max gave him a glass of hot tea to aid his decision and left Ari alone to ponder the situation. The local hole-in-the-wall restaurants were open now, and just for a moment Ari thought of going next door to buy a fresh bagel and cream cheese, since he had eaten nothing since yesterday's dinner, but the thought skated around the rim of his mind and disappeared as quickly as it had come. He was too fat anyway, and he could wait a while longer. So instead, he digested the text in front of him.

A grandmother in a pink jogging suit came in to buy a kiddush cup (wine cup for a special blessing) for a *bris* (circumcision) gift; a young couple spent an hour examining *mezuzot* (a container for a biblical blessing affixed to the doorpost of the home); and a black man wearing several heavy gold chains picked out a large, ornately designed *chai* representing the significant number eighteen. Sperling scratched his head.

Then a man wearing a beautiful leather and suede jacket carried in a large carton from Ralph's supermarket and slammed the front door angrily. The small silver bell attached to the door tinkled with agitation. The man wore designer jeans and a cashmere sweater with an intricate argyle pattern in shades of greys and blacks. He put the box on the glass counter with a thud. "*Goniffs*, thieves," he said to Max Sperling, when he came up to wait on him.

Ari Kremer tried to concentrate, but the conversation of the two men constantly interrupted him.

The stranger was clearly upset. His eyes shot fire, and his voice rose an octave with every sentence. "This is what I bought in Poland this summer," he said as he plunked a tissue-wrapped cylindrical object down on the counter with a bang. "Those *goniffs*, they'll cheat you every time."

Old Sperling looked from the man with the box to Ari, sitting at the back of the store studying his scrolls, and shrugged his shoulders and stroked his mangy beard as if to say, what do I need with a *meshuganah* like this?

Now Ari could see the man unwrap a Torah. The blue velvet mantle was embroidered with a silver *keter* (crown) on top of the tablets of Moses, guarded by the Lions of Judah.

"This," said the customer, "is what they showed me. Nice embroidery, right? Gives you the impression you're getting quality merchandise, right?"

Sperling nodded as the man took off the Torah cover, roughly laid it aside and began to unroll the scroll without first using a corner of a *tallis* to touch the Torah in a respectful ritual kiss. Max said a prayer to himself, then he reverentially touched the Torah.

"See, up to here the Torah looks good. I paid for it and sent it to California. I don't know much about these things, I hardly ever go to services myself, but I can recognize a Torah when I see one, and I thought I'd donate it to the synagogue in honor of my son's wedding. The velvet cover was in good condition and I thought the scroll would look nice in the ark with all the others. But those sons of bitches, look what they did to me." He unrolled several sections and lifted it up so Max could see the parchment, splotched with dark brown stains.

The shopkeeper again kissed the tips of his fingers and gently unrolled the Torah on top of the counter to examine it further. The customer became more agitated.

"*Goniffs,* I paid full price for this. It wasn't cheap, I can tell you. What do they do? They give me damaged goods. I didn't find out until I got the package home and opened it."

He leaned forward on the top of the glass counter and continued, "I've got a half-cousin still living in the town in Mannheim, Germany where I bought this. He's the one that said I could get a good deal from Malinowski, the dealer, in the first place. I had to go all the way to Heidleberg to see him and that's where he sold me the Leibowitz scroll. It had just come on the market."

The man tapped impatiently on the glass display case with a well-manicured nail, and a gold Rolex watch glinted on his wrist. He continued, "You know about this Torah? I asked my cousin. So my cousin says, 'Well, yes, it's common knowledge to the few Jews left here. But we don't talk about it much. No one wants to dredge up the past.' My cousin thinks that Malinowski kept it himself since the war and now that he needs a little money in his old age, he was looking for a buyer."

The customer's face was beginning to become red with anger and frustration, his words coming out faster and faster. "My cousin tells me that one Saturday morning in the Fall of '40, a certain Rabbi Leibowitz was sitting in front of the *bima* reading *Bamidbar*, whatever that is."

The Fourth of the Five Books of Moses, thought Ari, where the Jews are wandering in the wilderness. This customer doesn't know much.

"So Leibowitz was facing the ark, and in came the Nazis and they sprayed the synagogue with bullets. Half the congregation was dead or dying in their chairs, the other half screaming in terror. Men, women, little children. The rabbi was shot in the back, the words still in his mouth. He fell forward over the lectern that held the Torah, his blood spurting onto the parchment. It was this scroll.

"My cousin escaped along with a few others. As suddenly as it had happened, it was over. The soldiers left, shooting out the windows as they made their way out. The survivors helped bury the dead. They cleaned up what they could but the Torah was left where it was. One day it was simply gone. Malinowski probably buried it some place until now."

The customer had stopped his pacing and came to rest facing Max over the counter. "So you see I've been cheated." He paused, racking his brain to remember a word of Yiddish that might convey his opinion about the scroll. A word that might bring a bonding with the shop keeper, an acknowledgment of mutual heritage, so that Sperling would acknowledge how a fellow Jew had been robbed. "They pawned off a *schmustik* (dirty) Torah instead of the perfect one I thought it was. I don't want to give this bloody thing to my congregation. Why, the whole mood of the wedding would be taken down if they knew what had happened. They're coming to services to celebrate a joyous occasion; they don't want to remember the past. At least I don't want to be reminded of what a shitty world this is, I just want to get on with life. So I'm stuck, Mr. Sperling, and they tell me you're an honest man. What would you give me for it? Or maybe I can take it out in trade on another Torah?" He paused, "Like those nice, white ones I see lying on the counter back there."

Sperling said nothing but his eyes widened and his neck pulsed.

Suddenly Ari stood up. The young man's blood had run cold while he listened to the story, and he walked toward the front of the shop without being aware of what he was doing. The customer took Sperling's silence for resistance to buying damaged goods. The customer named his price, but because Sperling said nothing, the customer came up with a lower figure. He simply wanted to get rid of the terrible souvenir of war. Sperling started to say something, but the young rabbi approached the man. Ari had been trying to decide which Torah to buy, and now he had made up his mind. He took out his checkbook. "I'll pay your price," Ari said without a moment's hesitation, though he would have to add the money he had saved for the concordance to get the Torah. Surprised, the customer looked at the man in the baggy slacks and damp loafers and shrugged. Ari put his check on the table.

The man glanced at the check, eyelids flickering as though to say what kind of fool would buy this? "It's yours," he said with relief, put the Torah back in the grocery carton and pushed it toward Ari.

"I'm a little surprised that you bought that Torah." Sperling's eyes shone brightly at Ari after the customer left the shop. "First, because of its depressing history, second because it's damaged, and third because even though he lowered the price, it was still much more than you told me you could pay."

"Well," said the rabbi with a note of defiance in his voice, "I bought it precisely because of its history. The way I look at it the Torah isn't damaged, it's sanctified. And I think we all have to pay the price."

The sharp look Sperling cast on Ari was replaced by something else. "Yah," he said. "You chose well. It's a *shana heilega* (beautiful, holy) Torah."

❑

Rabbi Ari Kremer put the Torah in the back seat of his old blue convertible and drove home to the San Fernando Valley thinking about what had happened. He had gone off to buy something fine for the synagogue; he believed he was bringing them gold.

At services the next Saturday morning the new Torah sat in the *Oren Kodesh*, the ark. The lions and the crown, so thickly embroidered with gold and silver threads, seemed to give off a special glow. The roller tips wore silver pomegranates (donated by the Gendlemans), and little bells tinkled when it was taken out of the ark; its weight was light enough for the older members to dance with on *Simchas Torah*.

The Rabbi unrolled the scroll to the bloodstained text. His knees did not quiver that day, and he did not bother to use the stepping stool that Murray had placed by the *bima* for him. He felt very tall. His voice was strong and quavered with emotion, not weakness, as he delivered that morning's sermon.

His sermon was not as scholarly as it might have been had he purchased the concordance, and he had not had time to research the sayings of any major or minor authorities on the text. The notes he had prepared seemed to be nothing more than indecipherable bird tracks when he tried to read them. The words seemed meaningless. The congregation looked at him; some coughed and shuffled their feet as they waited expectantly. Two small children at the back of the room began to wiggle on their seats. A lady in a black coat blinked her eyes and woke up. So instead of his prepared sermon, he told the congregation of his hopes and dreams for the little synagogue, for all of them, himself included.

And he told them the story of why and how he had purchased this particular Torah for them. He painted word pictures of the aggrieved customer, and of what must have happened when Rabbi Leibowitz was shot, and how it was that the scroll found its way to America. Then he lifted up the Torah, made of wood light enough for the elderly to handle. "A *shana heilega* Torah," he said. And when he saw, for the first time, a light in the eyes of his audience, he suddenly knew he was the right man for the job. ❏

Succos is Coming

It was 1991, a sizzling September day, when I took my grandchildren out to the corn lady on Valley Circle Boulevard for palm fronds. It had been a politically tumultuous year what with the Gulf War a bare blip in our collective memory banks, trees tied up with yellow ribbons, and Russia—like London Bridge—was falling down. There were new drive-by shootings in Los Angeles and some crook had charged a trip to Mexico on my Visa card.

On the home front, Tammy, age three, threw up in the back seat of my car the day before, and the vomit that crawled down in the crevice in the back of the seat, had been rolled up into the seat belt housing. Five-year-old Rona left a Hershey bar on the back seat of my red Pontiac convertible. The seat was stained dark brown, and the car reeked from chocolate. A whiff of chocolate goes a long way, but when it is mixed with the faint cloying odor of vomit, it is unbearable.

Grandma, the baby sitter, like Willy Nelson, was out on the road again. The "Corn Lady" (also known as the "Strawberry Lady") had palm fronds piled up by her fruit and vegetable stand that would be perfect for the roof of the *succah*, a jerry-built structure we were going to construct in honor of the Jewish festival of the harvest. The *succah* was reminiscent of the temporary dwellings farmers in Israel had used since Biblical times when they worked in the fields. A *succah* looked very much like the corn lady's stall, I told the girls. The top was thatched with palms and other than that, open to the sky. I doubted that the corn lady would know anything about *Succos,* and I was hoping to scoop up all I needed for free.

The children were warbling in the back of the car about their great ideas for *succah* decorations. Shelly, age nine, was going to do an entire farm scene in red and blue, with possibly a giant orange sun and a bunch of corn. Rona was considering finger-painting with "only brown." They thought it would be cool to dress up Woof, their cousin's dog, and put makeup on her. Just a little blush and lipstick. Tammy, who was just getting the hang of great ideas, went along with everything by saying, "Me, too."

We stopped at the Corn Lady, and Rona was disappointed to find she was not actually made of corn. The woman, Flore, a young Mexican, smiled her gap tooth smile when she saw the children.

"You like corn today and strawberries?"

"Local?" I asked, looking at the small plot of cornfield we were standing in.

"Oh, no." She laughed. "We get ours from Oxnard. Oxnard grocery store," she laughed and priced out a dozen tender white ears. The kind I remembered as a child in Denver. Tiny perfect corn, popped in boiling water, freshly surrendering to our palates, real butter drenching every ear. Enough salt so you could still taste it on your lips when you had finished the corn. Mom would put a blue plate in the middle of the table for the empties, and I'd watch a pile of cobs piling higher and higher and higher.

I sighed. Today it would be just one ear apiece, slathered with some ugly yellow plastic soybean substitute made from partially hydrogenated soybean oil, water, salt, vegetable monos, diglycerides, soy lecithin, potassium sorbate, citric acid, artificial coloring and flavoring, betacarotine, and potassium sorbate with vitamin A palmtate added.

"These your grandchildren?" Flore handed me the corn.

How did she know? Didn't she think they were my kids? My hair was (artificially) dark and curly. I wore a size smaller than my daughter. People have a sixth sense about these things; they see so easily through the fantasies of oneself.

Actually, buying the corn was just a way of not calling attention to the fact that I really wanted the stack of palm fronds that stood against the small wood structure that sheltered the produce. I didn't want her to raise the price (if any) of the palm fronds. If she knew it was *Succos*, she might try to take advantage of the situation and charge me double or even triple for the palms. This way I could be casual, just ask her if she had any fronds, not assume she was selling them, just that I had noticed them and was inquiring. Inside the stand was a television and an air conditioner. Not the way my ancestors lived in the fields.

"Want a baby tomato?" Flore asked the girls who immediately backed away from her. They did not want to eat baby anything.

"I noticed you have old palm fronds over there," I said casually. "Are they going into the garbage? If so, I could take them off your hands for you.

"Oh, no," she said. "Believe it or not, I sell them at a good price."

What do you do with them?" I asked innocently.

"Sell 'em to Jewish guys," she said. "You know, *Succos* is coming."

❑

Crocodile Smile

THE ENTRANCE TO MEYER LIPINSKY'S CATERING HALL on Astoria Avenue in Forest Hills was flanked outside by twin walls of graffiti and inside by twin naked nymphette statues. The latter, encased for the occasion in gold quilted covers, resembled giant tea cozies. The nude figurines had been covered out of respect for the sensitivities of the guests arriving for the orthodox Jewish wedding. Yoni Silverman was marrying Aron Roth.

Meyer Lipinsky had, for reasons known only to himself, stocked his catering hall, not only with salmon, strictly kosher chicken and prime rib, but also with crocodiles, neither medium nor rare, but alive, on the hoof, so to speak.

The five living crocs were enclosed by a glass wall, ceiling to floor, in the upstairs foyer just to the right of the grand staircase. They eyed the tasty children as they made their way to the smorgasbord in the bride's reception room where they would soon fatten up.

The Lipinsky's had a molting interior in the last decade's style of excess. Every tassel had tassels. Anything that could be flossed, flecked, embroidered or gilded — was. The catering hall sported imitation antique mirrors liberally dappled with gold, and unsilvered splotches, dusty chandeliers with twenty-five concentric crystal circles, several creaking wood planked ball rooms. Windows draped in fading, threadbare velvet. Walls slightly peeling, embedded dirt at in the corners of the floors, carpeted rooms with wine spots and other unspecified stains. Instead of new carpet, Lipinsky bought new crocodiles and plastic palm trees for them to bask under.

The guests climbed the grand central stair case to visit the bride, Yoni Silverman as she held court in a separate room from her husband to be. She sat a few feet away from a long table laden with food.

Yoni's face had the placid look of someone who has given up control, who settles into a big easy chair, accepting the comfort it had to offer, even if she did not quite like the pattern of the upholstery. She was as talkative as cement, and hard pressed to come up with the fancy conversation required of a bride-to-be. She murmered "please," and "thank you," as she had been taught to do, and it was just as well since none of the guests who came to greet her expected anything more. They gave little tid-bits of advice, even if the pointers they passed on had not worked all that well.

The Orthodox rituals began with the bride and groom in their separate receiving rooms. That would be followed by the marriage ceremony, then an elaborate luncheon and folk danc-ing. Men and women did not dance together, each sex had its own circle. Both men and women were allowed to visit the bride before the ceremony, to dine on the smorgasbord and pay their respects, but only the men were invited to the groom's room, where Aron Roth and his gentlemen friends, scholars and the distinguished rabbis prayed, signed the *katubah* (wedding contract), drank *schnaps* and munched on sweet cakes. It was a much more decorous and learned atmosphere than the bride's reception room, where the bridesmaids grumbled under their smiles, that that their feet hurt.

Disembodied smiles floated; under mustaches, over bad teeth. Smiles that ran horizontally across the lower part of the face as though they were arrows stretched in a bow, ready for release. Smiles poached in Champagne. Smiles that sank quickly under the weight of party conversation, like small birds caught in quicksand. Smiles growing and fading, like shirts on the laundry line.

Men in dark suits of armor, dark ties plastered against white shirts, *yarmulkees*, a scattering of *peyes* (long curls running down the face in front of the ears), ritual fringes. The men moved slower than the women, were more serious, observed the food more than ate it, and drank the *schnaps.*

From the beginning there was some kind of internal tempo, as though everyone checked their individual rhythms at the door and merged in some mysterious way with the group and the beat. The air perspired. The children, on their frequent forays to the lobby, observed the reptiles dining on rats, possibly domestic.

Yoni Silverman was barely eighteen, and most of her friends were a year or two older. Her bridesmaids fretted about their dresses, the color of rusty nails. Pronounced hideous by the maids, another useless frock in their collection of dresses. Homely girls looked homelier, beautiful girls drained of color as though they had been sucked by a vampire. "Don't worry," the bridesmaids' moms said. "The dress can be taken in (or out), made longer (or shorter). Dyed a light pastel afterwards — or black. "Go, you'll have fun." Most didn't.

Yoni's parents had been married twenty-five years and lived in their Brooklyn home for twenty of them. Furniture; light bright woods, berber carpets, white walls, everything with history thrown out, decimated by the insatiable demands of the demon decorators. "Dark is dead, mahogany is out, Victorian dated," cried the interior decorators. They banished avocado green from the kitchen, scoured the bedroom of red cabbage roses, decimated the brick-a-brack, ripped out the shag, bundled the Grand Baroque sterling up and the tassled foot stools, the old amoires, and lace doilies. Aames chairs came in, along with steel sculpture, televisions with no doors to hide behind, Swavarksi crystal glistening in glass cabinets, The effect: stream-lined, boxy, contemporary. Drained.

Yoni's father, Leo, was a CPA and an opera buff, and her mother was a dental assistant part time. Their life revolved around the synagogue and the community and her younger brother, a diabetic. But Yoni was living an existence that didn't seem to require her to be in it. She felt like Sleeping Beauty, a princess in a glass coffin, waiting for the kiss of life.

The only person who excited her was cousin Zev, the son of her mom's sister. He was tall with flashing blue eyes, and hair black as evening shadows. He never said much, but she knew he watched her at family events. When their eyes met she looked away, but he stared on.

Last summer Zev was going to take his nine year old brother, Davey, to the Museum of Modern Art. Casually, he invited

Yoni to come along; making it seem like a favor to Yoni's mom to get her daughter out from under foot, and Mrs. Silverman agreed. The day was a blur. While Davey inspected the fountain in the central court, Yoni and Zev sat on a bench and talked. When Davey went to the bathroom, Zev and Yoni stood outside waiting. It was then that he suddenly and unexpectedly kissed her, pulling her towards him, putting his lips on hers, pressing her head gently to his and she was not at all surprised. She had rehearsed kissing on her pillow. Finding his embrace as familiar as it was sweet, she kissed him back with a fierceness he did not expect.

The skies did not fall in, the world did not speed up or slow down. Men and women dating, kissing, going off by themselves was just not done in her Orthodox community. They were breaking tradition, breaking the rules and nothing bad happened. Yoni wanted to stay in his arms, to explore his mouth with hers, never to leave him but Zev gently put her arms down.

"I'd better go in and get Davey," was all he said. Let the kid go pee by himself, she thought.

During the drive home they sat close together in the front seat, Davey fell asleep in the back. They talked about his school, his aspirations, his dreams. She spoke of things that she hadn't even known were on her mind, but somehow with him, it was easy to express her feelings. When they got home, he kissed her again before waking Davey. That kiss was deeper, his tongue in her mouth, the wetness of it, the fullness of it enticing, if she could have acted out her fantasies she would have taken off all her clothes but could not fantasize any further than that.

Through the year they continued to see each other at family celebrations. He took every opportunity to be near her. But by this time she had met Aron Roth, approved by her parents. She met Aron for tea in the lobby of the New York Hilton on Sunday afternoons, a favorite public yet private haunt of many Orthodox Jews. They spoke to each other for hours, but it was different than speaking with Zev. She and Aron never skated very deeply beneath life's surface. And when she had tried to tell him this, he didn't understand her, and she in turn, didn't understand herself. And then, in a bizarre defiance of her real feelings, Yoni pushed to become engaged to Aron.

"It couldn't hurt to wait a year, you're only eighteen," her mother pleaded. "What would it hurt if you waited a little?"

What would it hurt? Yoni was determined to do exactly the opposite of what her parents said was best for her. Secretly, they had counted on that. Yoni knew they would never agree to her marrying her first cousin, Zev, even though it was permitted under Jewish law. Under American law, in some states, it was prohibited. "And anyway," her father said, "we don't need any more nuts in the family."

There was nothing at all wrong with Aron, he was a perfectly nice guy from a nice family in Queens, reasonably attractive and quite smitten with her. She agreed to the marriage even though she knew she was going directly from the house of her parents to Aron's without having the feeling, save for that one day with Zev, that she had ever lived. The force of life moved beyond Yoni's control.

Today she was going to marry Aron, but the face she sought in the crowd was Zev's.

Nessa, Yoni's mom, was angry at her mother, Miriam for being late to the wedding. Grandma had not come in yet from the Bronx, which was under most traffic conditions, not more than forty-five minutes away.

Yoni sat on a chair in her receiving room smiling congenially at everyone who came up to take a photo of her. It was a pleasant experience; her mind was on hold while Aunts and uncles, cousins and friends paid their respects.

Ten minutes before the ceremony, a taxi drew up to the front door of the catering establishment and a tiny beaked woman with a face that could mangle cats, stepped out.

"We've been roaming Brooklyn," Miriam explained to her daughter Nessa. "I had a Jamaican driver who seemed to be under strict orders to only ask directions from people who were just as dumbfounded as he was about the direction to Forest Hills. Two hours in the car, and here we are."

❑

Rabbi Marvin Decklebaum, the groom's uncle, performed the ceremony. The bride, resplendent in a long sleeved, high necked gown, did the *sheva brochas* (seven blessings) walking around the groom seven times attended by her mother and mother-in-law. The ring was placed on the appropriate finger. Yoni and Aron sipped wine, Aron broke the wine glass, and before she knew it the ceremony was over and she felt herself to be on the edge of unexplored territory.

"I wish your grandpa could have seen this," Miriam said to her granddaughter after the ceremony as she was ushered along with the rest of the crowd to the sit-down luncheon. Miriam eyed her matzah ball soup suspiciously. "Wouldn't be surprised if they made this out of old crocodiles," she sniffed to no one in particular. No sooner was the soup served, hotter than the day outside, than the band began its head splitting music. The sound bounced of the walls so that the effect was like being inside of a microphone rather than outside. Old people turned off their hearing aides and heard the sounds with a clarity they hadn't enjoyed in years.

Although the guests could go over to either circle to watch, mostly women watched the women's circle dance and men crowded around the men's circle. Yoni had fasted all morning until the wedding luncheon, was brought into the center of the women's circle by her girl friends, and then surrounded by them as they danced the hora. The married women that danced felt their scalps damp under their *shaidels* (wigs).

The young women kept their eyes on the bride. Beautifully wrapped packages they were, in silks and lace. And while they danced, they wondered, when will it be me? When will it be my turn? Mothers, grandmothers, mothers-in-law, sisters, cousins and friends danced as women guests joined in and left at intervals. Around and around they all went; variations on a theme.

The men danced harder and more loudly than the women, took turns pantomining a mock bull fight. Finally, the groom and the bride were raised up on chairs and placed on the participants' shoulders. The couple "danced" in the air while still seated on the chairs, connected to each other by a handkerchief.

A half hour later and the music was still blasting. Yoni's mom propelled herself forward to dance with her daughter. They held hands and twirled around spinning faster and faster. Nessa locked gazes with her daughter and the two of them spun like a bright constellation, ever faster, ever more dizzing pace. Miriam watched from her place at the table, wanting to dance with her daughter and granddaughter. Wanting to tell them both something, something about life, something about husbands, something she should have said long ago.

Nessa and Yoni looked at each other as they danced, looked through each other, into each other as though their individual lives no longer existed. The bride in white, mother in blue. Their lines blurred and colors fused till at last the guests could discern hardly more than a light pastel foam glistening in the center. As the women sped up their already rapid dance steps, each became aware of their own lives as though they were spinning in some kind of giant centerfuge. The daughter saw her future in her mother; marriage and children, life in the Jewish community, holidays and study — and perhaps something different than her mother, though at that precise moment, Yoni didn't know what that difference would be.

Nessa spun without restraint, as though all the boundaries of her life were melting to the sweet horns and shuddering violins of the band. Beads of sweat under her arms blotted the blue fabric of her sequinned dress, but still she danced, remembering her own wedding.

Suddenly, as she danced, Nessa felt as though she could see through the walls of the room, past the guests and the dancing and the tables of food. Past the schnaps and into the walls to the crocodile's glass enclosure. Why in the world did Lipinsky keep these reptiles?

She imagined she could hear the crocodiles singing their bad-tempered songs. Crocodiles do not eat old ladies, she thought. They wait for something tastier to come along. She could see their evil skin with tread marks like old tires. Ah, she knew the crocodile well. She had always fancied one lay in her bed separating her from her husband. If it was not a crocodile, then what was it that came between her and the man who slumbered nearby? Something occupied that gap between them so that they felt oddly injured when they came up against each other.

In her mind's eye, she saw the crocodile opening his mouth, inconsiderate teeth shining, eyes gleaming with droop lidded suspicion. The crocodile comes with the bed, she thought, though no salesman ever sold him, it comes with the bed the way mold is carried by growing things that have stopped growing. So the crocodile is carried invisibly, ready for the seasons of the bed.

The first season the bed is empty, the couple has not yet found each other and the crocodile waits. The second season the couple, having met, try each other out and the crocodile smiles. The third season, the crocodile has advanced, the lovers know too much of one another, small wounds gather. The crocodile advances to the center of the bed by the fourth season when the couple sleeps each on their own side, remembering the second season in dreams. The crocodile eases down the center of the bed and sings.

When crocodiles sleep, they make good pets and warm the available space, doing only what they have been trained by the couple to do — that's why everybody keeps them.

❏

Nessa felt like throwing up. Too much wine. With every revolution of the circle she saw different faces of her past. Mother and daughter, daughter and mother, for an instant a combined being. Mother stopped dancing, begged to be excused, saidshe was too tired. Yoni sat down next to Miriam, needing a cool drink.

When Nessa came back from the lady's room a few minutes later, she joined her daughter. Both were wringing wet. Each kicked off their shoes under the table to relieve their pulsing feet. Miriam, Nessa and Yoni knew they had been swept up in the cycle of life that would be repeated over and over again, with or without them, and that a wedding is the season when crocodiles smile.

❑

The Handkerchief Mouse

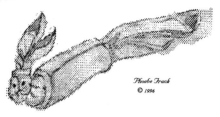

Phoebe Frank
© 1996

UNCLE TEDDY WAS A BRIGHT RELIEF to the rest of our rather dour family. He was a handsome man with thick, curly red hair. "Even if he wears rags, he looks like a prince," my mom said. "If you grow up to be a man like him, Marty, you'll be trouble." My uncle was aristocratic-looking with burning blue eyes and an smile that careened off to the left followed by his nose hovering in the same direction. When Uncle Teddy smiled at you, you felt gift wrapped.

In a world where Mom's chief worry was how to get through the Depression after my dad died, Teddy's concern was how to become a movie star.

At eight I helped my mom in the small grocery store my Dad had bought on the south side of Chicago. I worked behind the counter after school, taking down the cans from the highest shelf with a stick that had two pincers at one end. I wondered if I could use it to pick up the girls' dresses (without their knowing it) so that I could see the mystical crack through their underpants. The only person I dared tell these thoughts to was Uncle Teddy, who said with a wink, "If you try it, let me know what happens."

Teddy Karasick was a bum. A *bumski,* my mother said; she thought that word made him sound even worse than he was. "A *fafoofnick* who *schmies* around all day."

He wasn't a *schmier,* he was a *tummler* every summer in the Catskills. Today he'd be a warm-up for the main attraction. Winters he worked the family *simchas.* "Folks, I wanna tell ya something," he would say, sounding just like Bob Hope. And whatever he wanted to tell, they would listen. His favorite saying was, "the road to good intentions is paved with Hell."

I remember, just before he left Chicago for L.A., that he would do close-up magic in our living room. Sweat rolling down his brow, he would make coins sprout from your nose and the cleavage of fat cousin Zelda's breast and even from under Aunt Trude's *sheitle.* Uncle Teddy had just come home from World War II and was starting to get back on his feet again.

My Mom told me, just before she died a few months ago, that Uncle Teddy was in a nursing home in L.A. She described how Teddy had begged their parents to give him singing lessons, but they, being from the old country did not take to the idea. Even if they had, there was no money for it. They signed him on instead to apprentice at Mr. Baum's bakery to feed the fire and smack the dough. By comparison with Teddy, who detested his work, I had it easy in the grocery store.

Maybe you don't remember during World War II how they rationed sugar, flour, butter and eggs. Mr. Baum's business went down and he had to lay off people. Just about that time, my uncle decided to enlist and had to get parental consent because he was under age. It was that or singing lessons, he said, so his folks signed the paper. Uncle Teddy hoped he could get into the entertainment services, work with the Red Cross and the USO shows, but they sent him to school and he came out the other end a tail gunner flying over Europe.

Well, he got shot down over Europe, landed in occupied territory, and was a P.O.W. for two years. The only way he survived, he said, was by inventing the mouse. He made it out of a handkerchief that he twisted and knotted in a certain way, and as to this day, I've never seen another one.

He did sleight-of-hand and tricks with the mouse in exchange for food, and put on little performances to keep up his comrades' spirits up. One day the war was over and Uncle Teddy came back.

He was a lot quieter than before. He was not so quick to laugh or tell a joke, and when he came into a room it seemed as though he would always take a step back, rather than forward. His hair was a lot thinner now, a rusty smear on the top of his head. When he looked at you, he looked off to the side as though there were terrible things in his head that he couldn't speak of, things that waste a man and let him know he'll never get to where he wanted to go when he was a dreamy-eyed kid.

When he came home, there wasn't much call for tail gunners in Chicago, and the bakery was long out of business. So he got a conductor job on the Ravenswood El and he pretty much did that until he left to try his fortune in Hollywood. Uncle Teddy knew he had no talent for anything except illusion.

Thinking back on it, I believe I first really became aware of Uncle Teddy when he came back from the war. I remember his dark uniform and the conductor's hat that he wore when he got off work.

One day my uncle asked, "Want to know what got me through that damn prison, Marty, eh?"

Who could resist a line like that, especially when you're a boy who never came near the war except to duck under my school desk in practice air raid drills? My father was a ward captain and wore an armband, and a real helmet, and he was in charge of the blackout. And sometimes I went with him and we made sure that not the slightest bit of light shone out through the heavily curtained windows, and that everybody was following instructions.

Now my uncle asked me if I wanted to know the secret of how he survived, and this was more exciting than Captain Marvel, (Shazam!) and Billy Batson, and Lois Lane and Superman combined. I had already heard something about the mouse and I didn't understand it, so I said, "Sure, how'ja do it?"

"This," he said pulling out a fine white cotton handkerchief from his pocket, the kind everyone carried back then. It was essential equipment. You could wipe your shoes, or wrap leftover lunch, or mop up a girl's tears with it.

I had a pocket hanky with my initials on it (which embarrassed me very much), especially since it came with its fellows in a splendid dozen-in-the-pack, given to me one year by my an ever- practical aunt for Chanuka. Can you imagine a gift like that when you wanted a set of Lionel trains? And instead you got something to blow your nose on? And my mother washed those handkies by hand! Can you imagine? I thought such a boring, plain, tidy gift matched the quality of our unimaginative, boring lives.

So where was I? Yes — Uncle Teddy pulled out his handkerchief and began to fold it this way and that, that way and this and I kept asking him what he was doing.

And he said, "Just wait," as he folded, wrapped and twisted it, not looking at it once during the process, but keeping his eyes focused on me.

Shazam! Suddenly a kind of tube lay in his hand with a length of material coming out of each end. It looked like the cylindrical paper party favors you pulled on and they made a sharp cracking noise. "Crackers," we used to call them.

Then, Alakazam, he tied in a small knot in one end and suddenly there were two ears with the knot forming the face. The other end of the tube became the tail. He took a pen and put two dots where eyes should be, and a handkerchief mouse nestled in the palm of his hand.

It was amazing how he did it. Manipulating the handkerchief and talking all the while, not even looking at what he was doing, but holding me in the grip of his fierce blue eyes, he created the "Mouse of Oaken." This is the mouse that had saved his life. Oaken was the name of the town where he had been taken prisoner, or at least that's as near as he ever came to the correct pronunciation of the word.

"Want to pet it?"

Well, heck, I knew it wasn't real, and it was hard to believe this toy had saved his life, but it was even harder to oblige my uncle and reach down to touch it.

But Teddy Karasick, he with the dizzying smile, never did anything to embarass me, so I decided to humor him in that grown-up way that wise children adopt when dealing with their demented and misguided parents.

I reached out to touch the thing (it was after all, just a rolled handkerchief), and Crimminy Pete if that mouse didn't jump forward right along my uncle's outstretched arm. "COME ON!" I said.

It startled me so, I nearly thought it alive. And Teddy put it back in the palm of his hand and challenged me to touch it again and once more the mouse dashed forward along his arm and my Uncle had to retrieve it.

"How'ja do that?"

"I told you he was my pal, didn't I" Teddy asked. And I could only mumble, "Yes," stupefied as I was by the hanky mouse that seemed to have a life of its own.

"Can I try?" and he put the mouse in the palm of my hand, but it refused to move. It moved all right in Teddy's hand, and I was disappointed. "Howja do it?" I pleaded with the desparation of a child who KNOWS that what is about to be learned is something that, inexplicably, will change the course of his life. I HAD to know the secret of the "Mouse of Oaken," that single-handedly had saved my Uncle's life, and it undoutedly would save mine in some future unspecified time and place.

I asked him many times over the next year to teach me the trick but Teddy just said, "Only one mouse to a family." One day, however, just before Teddy was about to leave on his Hollywood adventure, he came over for a small family birthday party I was about to have.

"And what would you like for a present, Marty?" he asked with a sly smile, as if he didn't know.

"The mouse," I cried. "The Mouse of Oaken."

"I told you only one mouse to a family — in any city," he added. "And as I'm leaving town, I guess you can take over this city for me," and he blinked that meadering smile of his. "Hollywood is my new territory."

That night he taught me how to make the mouse. You started with a man's pocket square, folded it into a triangle, rolled it up, turned it over, ah but this is something you have to see to learn.

"I wouldn't want the secret to die with me," he said while he watched my awkward attempts to produce the perfect rodent. It looked so easy in his hands.

"After two years in a prison camp practicing day and night, even in the dark, it would be easy for you, too," he said, encouraging me even as I turned out dozens of misfit mice. None worthy to bear the name of the the Mouse of Oaken.

He showed me a hundred times if he showed me once, and even drew little diagrams for me to follow. "Failure is a repeat performance only if it's the last one," he said. "Because it only takes one success to wipe out losing."

"Honest to God, I'll get it right," I said struggling not to produce runty rodents.

"I know you will, kid, and you'll show me when you visit me in L.A. I'll send for you when I'm a star, and you'll have it down pat by then."

I kissed this funny, charming man goodbye thirty years ago and promised to see him soon. But he never sent for me or became a movie star. Mom said he got a job on the old Red Car trolleys in Los Angeles, and I was sure he was amusing his passengers with the mouse.

For weeks after Uncle Teddy left I sat at the dinner table and practiced, but produced only still-born mice. Some were pathetic one-eared creatures, some had ears at both ends, and sometimes tails grew where ears should have been. Much of the time the mouse unraveled in my hand as I worked. All I had to show for the hours I put in was a pile of wrinkled handkerchiefs and sharp looks from Mom and Dad.

It took a month of trying before I produced a mouse worthy of eyes. One day I finally got the process right and began turning out perfect mice. I used up all my of handkerchiefs and startled my folks by asking for more on for my birthday. I began to practice at night, in the dark when I was supposed to be asleep. Not only were my mice beginning to be sleek specimens, I was determined to make them like Teddy—without looking.

Then I had to learn to make the mouse move along my outstretched arm. You could not cock your wrist, or hold your arm at an angle. Just rest your arm on the edge of a table, perfectly straight, and tickle the mouse's rear with the right hand. When I learned to do it right, the audience's eye was directed toward the hand stroking the mouse. When I did it well, the mouse looked like it was moving of its own accord.

I often thought how great it would be to show how well I did the mouse to Uncle Teddy in Hollywood, but I wasn't to see him again until years later.

In the meantime, I used the mouse to make friends on the playground and later as an icebreaker at parties, and at dinners and finally when I married, I entertained the children and eventually the grandchildren with it. Unlike Uncle Teddy, I taught mouse construction and training to anyone who asked.

I even began to pack extra cotton hankies on holiday trips, for everyone wanted to keep one. Everywhere I went, mice proliferated and with them the laughter and shocked surprize that they provoked.

And the Mouse of Oaken did change my life. You cannot remain shy with a mouse running down your sleeve.

Just a few months ago I had to go to L.A. to do some voice-over commercials. I had gotten out of the grocery store business, because I had learned from the mouse that I could be funny, and charming and witty and wise and I found my place in life that kind of thing. I'm not a big star, but I like what I'm doing.

I found the address mom had given me for Uncle Teddy and decided to look him up to thank him for the special thing he did for me those thirty or forty long years ago. "You were always his favorite," I remember mom saying. "Things are not so good for him, now."

I expect, I said to myself, that Uncle Teddy will make me a mouse even better than what I can do, and even if he lives in a retirement home, the folks there will chuckle, and Teddy himself will be the star performer. In fact I imagined him in the center of an adoring circle of seniors performing sleight-of-hand and mouse tricks. Perhaps he had even relented and taught them all to make the wondrous little rodents, and I imagined a roomful of performing handkerchief mice.

When I was finished with my business in Los Angeles, I drove out to see him. He was sitting in a bathrobe the day I saw him and just for a moment he still looked like a prince. The old jagged smile still there, but the teeth were more yellow, and a front one was missing. His hands were a little shakey, and his eyes a bit rheumy, and he tried but couldn't quite remember who I was until I told him. "How's your father," he asked, and it tore me up because Dad had died around the time Ted went to enlist in the army.

He was strapped with a seat belt into an easy chair with a tray on it, like an adult high chair. To keep him from falling out and hurting himself, the nurse explained later. I looked around the room; several others sat in the same contraption. The television was tuned to Phil Donahue or something, and most of the group seemed hypnotized rather than involved by the program—and there wasn't a mouse in sight. True to his word, I guessed, uncle Teddy kept the secret of mouse making to himself.

"Uncle Ted," I said, "I meant to tell you a long time ago how much I loved the Mouse of Oaken, how hard I worked to learn it, and how much joy its brought me and everyone who's seen it. I'm so grateful you taught me how to make it."

My uncle looked at me, with a quizzical lift to his eyebrow. "Mouse," he said, and patted me as though I were a sweet, demented child to be humored. "What mouse?"

Uncle Teddy had given away a part of himself to me, and had forgotten all that it had meant to him. And as I left him that day, I felt in some deep way, that now I was the true custodian of the Handerkerchief Mouse.

❑

Phoebe Frank
© *1996*

The Room of Mirrors

THE TUTTLES LIVED NEXT DOOR AT 457 SOUTH HIGH STREET for less than a year. They came and went as swiftly as black crows across the fields, and for a long time after they had gone, I missed them the same way I'd miss my Boy Scout knife if I'd lost it because it too, could heal or cut or do both at the same time.

The Tuttles were a white haired couple, surprisingly spry for their age. Perhaps a hundred or a thousand years old, we kids thought. Anyone over seventeen was really ancient and by that standard the Tuttles were probably friends of T-rex.

I'm Jason Kelly. When I was a boy I had a basketball shaped face and pink cheeks that looked like they were scrubbed with a wire brush. But the rest of me was strangely lanky, as though head and body were not made for each other and they were waiting for permission to unite. I was thirteen years old and had a shiny Schick razor sleeping in my dresser drawer waiting for its cutting time. Daily, I inspected the landscape above my lip for a crop to mow down, but the space lay fallow.

We lived in Denver, Colorado. It was sometime in the mid 40's when Gold Star Families hung banners in their windows to show how many sons had been killed in the war. What with bomb drills and war bond drives, fear sucked at us like ticks.

Me and the guys my age couldn't wait to grow up so we could enlist and fight them Krauts, 'n Japs, 'n Italians but we were stuck on the home front and all we could do to help was save fat in cans. We'd get little red tokens, when we turned the tins in to the butcher, and if we'd saved up enough we'd get an extra ration of meat.

There was a sign at the ritzy Brown Palace restaurant that said, "Please do not ask for a second pat of butter."

"For the war effort," my folks explained.

We collected newspapers at school. I never understood what the Army would do with fat and newspapers. Maybe they needed butter for their toast when they read the funnies.

❑

The Tuttles had an old chow dog with a black tongue that they used to take for walks along Cherry Creek. The locals pronounced it like "Cheracrick." All one word spat out fast like you were stepping on an insect.

I met the Tuttles when I was taking orders for greeting cards I was selling for my Boy Scout Troop. I knocked on their front door and introduced myself. "Hi, I'm Jason Kelly and our Troop could make a little money if you'd like to buy these cards".

"Try to look intelligent and friendly when you're selling," my father said.

I tried to do both, and maybe I succeeded, because Mrs. Tuttle bought two boxes, when she had only wanted to buy one. "Ed, come here, she called to her husband," and he sprang like a panther to the door. "Looks like Charles, doesn't he"

Her husband looked me over and said, "Uhm." And they raised their eyebrows and looked at each other like they wanted to talk about something but couldnt think how to do it in front of me. Instead, they said they were going to decorate their house for Halloween, which was coming up in a week or two, and asked me if I'd like to help.

Right then they invited me to sit down on their front porch swing, and gave me a glass of lemonade just like I was grown-up company. From that time on they were real friendly and said I could swing anytime. I invented all kinds of stories while I sat in that swing skimming over the creaky floor boards. I would swing as high as I could, wondering if I could swing high enough to touch the ceiling or maybe even the sky.

One day while I was day-dreaming on the Tuttles' swing, Mrs. T called me in for a lemonade refill. The house had a cabbage odor, and as I passed through the living room to the kitchen, I noticed the picture of a boy about my age on the mantle piece, along with some other photographs.

"Oh, that's Charles at your age," Mrs. T said when she saw me stop for a moment to look.

Charles-at-my-age had a big moon face and a kind of startled expression like he was trying to say something but couldn't. I must have wrinkled my brow thinking these people were too old to have such a young child, because Mr. T, who was sitting on a mustard and green plaid sofa, picked up another picture to show me. "This one is Charles in the Air Force.

The photograph showed a young man leaning against a B-29. I didn't hardly see much of Charles-at-my-age in the Charles-in-the-Air-Forces face, but his eyes cast the same undecipherable message. Then I looked up at the mantle and saw a gold star on a white field with a red border and suddenly understood that Charles had died in the war.

Over Germany, Mrs. Tuttle said, just as though I had asked her where Charles-in-the-Air-Force had died. She started to say more, but Mr. Tuttle put his hand on my shoulder, and guided me back onto the porch.

"The wife gets upset," he said, going down the front porch steps and over to a wheel-barrel that was standing near by filled with different size pumpkins. In the middle was the biggest pumpkin I had ever seen. "I dont want her to get started or I'll never hear the end of it. You know how it is."

But I didn't.

"Charles enlisted. We tried to tell him to wait 'til the draft called him up, but he wanted to get in the fight while the getting was good. We told him to wait 'til the war came to him, but he wouldn't." Mr. T put the pumpkin on his front porch and put a lot of newspapers under it. "He was a pilot. Plane got hit and he went down with it."

I could see Charles, as played by Humphrey Bogart, going down in flames, still shooting at the enemy with his machine gun. At the last minute, he crawls through the body of the airplane, and takes over the controls from the dead pilot—Van Johnson. They land safely and the two heros walk away from the flaming wreckage and laugh. The thrilling vision made me want to run away from home and enlist right then.

Mr. T saw my excitement and said nothing.

"Can I help carve the pumpkin?" I asked to kind of get things going again between us.

There must have been millions of seeds inside. I used my Boy Scout knife to scrape the walls of the pumpkin, loosening the seeds. The slimy mush was cool to the touch. Hundreds of pale beige seeds slipped through my fingers, like they were slithery living beetles. We worked on that pumpkin for hours, scraping out all the rind and then separating the seeds from the pulp. He washed and dried the seeds in the sun and Mrs. T baked them in oil, salted them and said I'd get some on Halloween. We didn't talk about Charles again.

Mr. T's pumpkin face had off-center eyes that seemed to follow you as you walked by it, and the nose triangle was too big. There were made sharp-looking teeth inside the mouth that curved down like a scream. Even by day, without a candle, that Jack-O-Lantern sent cold chills up and down my spine.

Me and the other kids looked forward to bringing brown paper shopping bags to each house, to collect Hershey bars, Bit-O-Honeys, Three Musketeers, cider and homemade cookies. And the only thing bad that happened to your candy was that your parents ate all the good stuff after you went to bed. Grownups were afraid of the kids' tricks, not the other way around.

A few days before Halloween I brought over the two boxes of greeting cards that the Tuttles had ordered, and Mrs. Tuttle gave me some freshly squeezed lemonade and homemade Nestle Chocolate Chip Cookies for my trouble. "Chocolate chip was Charles's favorite," she said.

I kept on chewing.

"I once had a dream when Charles was your age, that he was born and died in a year. Grew from an infant to full manhood in one year. Everything he did, we applauded because he did it so fast and so easy. At the end of that year he died with a full white beard. What do you think of that?"

"Now, now, don't bother Jason with such thoughts. There's nothing we could have done to stop him." Mr. T had ripples in his forehead.

I wouldn't mind fighting the war, I thought. Jeez, it would be great flying a plane, being a hero, shaving. I swallowed my cookies, swigged down the drink and decided it was time to go home.

❑

The old couple hung jangly cardboard skeletons from the beams on the front porch and they danced when the wind blew.

"Baby stuff," I thought to myself. "That's not scary."

Mrs. T tied Indian corn, all purple and rust and golden, to the front door and I helped her hang black and orange crepe paper streamers all around the house. Then she and I made a ghost from an old bed sheet draped on wire hangers that we set in the living room's big front window. "Since you made it, you won't be afraid of it, right, Jason?"

'Course I wasn't scared, 'till she asked me that question.

The neighborhood kids couldn't help but notice the big production going on. We'd sit huddled together on the porch swing and whisper endlessly about the Tuttles preparations. And the big question was, since they didn't have children, why they were doing it? I lorded it over them by showing off how much I knew about the Tuttles. "They once had a kid named Charles," I said. Maybe they're making Halloween for him.

Wednesday before Halloween, the crackling bright October days were beaten out by unusually mean weather. A drizzling rain started in, and a raw and wicked wind kicked up that chilled the hearts of all the girls who were going to wear Miss-Bathing-Beauty and fairy princess costumes. Moms would make them wear long woollies under their outfits, or big sweaters over them and the girls fretted about how they would look. There were a lot of tears from ballerinas who'd rather die, cold and blue, in their tutus than wear warm clothes.

Most costumes were simple homemade affairs. A ghost was a good costume because you could throw a sheet over your jacket and still look great. Raggedy Ann was a favorite, and the big deal was to get a colored mask at the dime store that covered your eyes and part of your nose. Some kids got store bought costumes made from sleazy, shiny cloth that cost maybe two dollars. The material couldn't be washed because the sizing would melt and the fabric would be ruined if you got it dirty (and you always did); you would have to get a new costume next year. We loved this because we always wanted new costumes, and the Moms hated it because every year they had to spring for another outfit.

I hate to say it, but that Halloween I went as a clown. Although it wasn't homemade (which counted in my favor), I had wanted Superman, but they didn't have any left in my size. Clowns were babyish. It was tough toenails for a kid in a clown costume. And everyone knew Superman could beat up anybody he wanted to, while clowns were stupid. So I should have felt good in a real store-bought costume, but instead the costume put me in a bad mood for Halloween. When it's hard for your folks to cough up money enough for your outfit, you can't complain. So I kept my mouth shut and silently vowed I would have a growth spurt next year and then Alan, my younger brother, would have to wear it, not me. Then I'd make sure to get to the store early for Superman or maybe a soldier or sailor uniform.

❑

The Tuttles' house stood all decorated like the witch's cottage in Hansel and Gretel and when they were finished, the Tuttles put a sign up on their front door now that said, **Halloween House.** But instead of being adorned with gingerbread cookies, a real skeleton danced in the face of a cold wind. I couldn't imagine where they had got that from and it made me think I'd stay clear of the place on Halloween night.

Wednesday night I looked out of my bedroom window and could see the side of the Tuttles' house through a row of lilac bushes. In spring the lilacs were as purple and dark as blood, and they had a deep fruity smell that made the bees pause in their buzzing. But right now, all that was on my mind was to try to peer through the naked bush. I could see right into their kitchen and since their windows were open, I could even smell the strange aromas that wafted out. Huge pots were boiling, boxes of strange, unidentifiable objects sat huddled on the table. One of them was moving! It looked to me like a black cat. Cripes! I had been over to their place lots of times but I had never noticed a cat. Were they going to boil her? I gave up looking, hopped in bed, and finally fell asleep with the thought of dead cats roaming around in my dreams. I vowed not to go to the Tuttles on Halloween night.

Thursday dawned a little brighter than the preceding days,

though it was still unusually raw outside. None of the kids could eat supper that night and parents usually let them off easy with a hot dog or something quick. Alan wanted to start out at the Tuttles but Mom thought it might be too scary for him to go there. She never said a word about me going, though I kind of wished she had.

Kids Alan's age generally started out around seven, before the stars were out. Kids like me began our rounds at eight or nine, and the older gang went out about ten. Alan was going to be the Lone Ranger. He had on a pair of old white pants, a holster, a plaid shirt, and a dime store cowboy hat. Mom penciled a mustache above his lips. "Makes you look more like the sheriff, " Dad said. If I got home early enough I'd have time to swipe a few things from Alan's bag before I went to bed.

Early Halloween evening, Mr. Tuttle set up a phonograph player on the front lawn, and ran a long extension cord through on open window into the house and blasted the porch with creepy music from *Night on Bald Mountain*. There was a kind of urgent undertone to the score that made my skin crawl. The old chow dog sitting on their porch didn't like it either and left in a huff.

The more I thought about it the better it seemed to be to leave the Tuttles for last, and then I could decide if I wanted to go.

I went out alone and met up with Toot Bishop. Toot had the same stupid clown suit as me, and we both felt dumb about it, so we banded together in misery. He was fat and everybody knew the clown costume was the only one that would fit him.

We worked the neighborhood like pros and stayed clear of the high school gang that started making their rounds. Sometimes they'd take your candy bag, or rip holes in it so your stuff would drop out. Sometimes they'd just try to scare you. Whatever the big guys did to us, we did to the little kids. We couldn't wait to grow up so we could mangle everybody else.

The fun was to trade stuff after each house and compare what each person got. We didn't like "Bit-O-Honeys" too much 'cause they took too much time to eat and they made your teeth stick together. Hershey bars were the best 'cause you could chomp them down quick and be ready for more. Toot was eating his supplies as fast as he got them and by the time we got near the Tuttles, he dropped out to throw up. Lucky for him, it went all over the front of his clown suit and that meant for sure he could get a new costume next year. That left me alone in front of the Halloween house, listening to that weird music with chocolate rumblings in my stomach, wondering if I should go in.

When I set foot on that porch the old floor boards creaked like crazy, and the skeleton bones danced up a storm. Ten flickering Jack-O-Latterns stood on the porch rail, and their eyes watched me as I rang the doorbell. No one came. I knocked. Nothing happened. That was pretty mean, I thought. No one home?

Then the door opened (more creaking) and Mr. Tuttle appeared. He didn't wear a costume, just a black sweater and pants and he carried a flashlight held under his chin that made the light billow over his face. His eyes looked like the huge hollows of rotting trees. His wispy hair stood up on end, and his voice sounded like Raymond, the host on the *Inner Sanctum* radio show.

"Good evening," he said, just exactly like Raymond. "We've been expecting you. Thought maybe you weren't coming." He made it seem like he was waiting for me, special. The living room in back of him was draped in black crepe paper I had helped hang, and Mr. T's face seemed to float in the air above his dark clothing. I was afraid that if I reached out to touch him, there'd be only air. The same pictures were still on the mantle, watching.

"Ready for some fun?" Mr. T asked, guiding me down the hall. "I see you've got a clown costume tonight, Jason. Charles had exactly the same one at your age."

That made me want to throw up. "I hate it," I said, spluttering out the truth. "It's a baby costume and I hate it" I didn't want Mr. T to think that being a clown was my choice. I want to wear what the older kids wear. If I was older right now I could be in the army and if I was in the army, all I would want to do is kill, kill, kill. The first one I'd kill would be that stupid Charles.

"I know," was all he said.

He didn't try to make me feel OK about being a clown (like my mom would) but walked me to a dark room. Then he asked if I was ready for the blindfold and though my heart stopped beating and I felt like a block of ice, I said, "Yes."

"I didn't know I'd have to be blindfolded or I wouldn't have come," I told myself.

"Yes, you knew, you clown creep," something else inside of me said.

Mr. Tuttle put the blindfold on me and took my trick-or-treat bag and told me he'd hold it for me. Well, the candy might be safe, but what about me? I could feel ice hollows of sweat rolling across my brow. Somehow wearing the blindfold made me more aware of the sounds around me. *Night on Bald Mountain* scratched its way through my brain.

"Now just put your hand in here," the old man said and guided my hand into a deep pail filled with little round things, all cold and slimy like. "Sheep eye balls," he said. "Want to eat one?"

The thing fell from my hand. "Eggs," I told myself, "Just shelled, hard-boiled eggs."

"And here we have worms, Jason. Yummy, yummy." And he plunged my hand in a tepid dish of long, squiggly things. Mr. Tuttle laughed in his Raymond voice. "They'd make nice eating, too. Try one!"

'Course I knew they was just spaghetti. But how come they were moving?

Mr. Tuttle was quiet.

Then something wispy, like hair or cobwebs, touched my face. I hadn't remembered hanging anything like that! And then Mr. T placed one of my hands into something warm, the other into icy liquid and it felt really weird. "Just blood," said Mr. T.

"Just water," I thought. "This is duck soup." What had I been worried about?

The Tuttles had a few other tricks. I went through each of them feeling a curious mixture of relief and disappointment because I could figure out how they did everything. And I hinted as much to the old man when he told me I could take off my blindfold.

"Ah," Mr. T said in that oily Raymond-voice. "You seem a little let down, Jason. Perhaps you'd like to see—something special?"

I felt as though he was reading my mind. I was at a loss for words, trying to decide what to do, when I suddenly realized I was standing alone in a dark room.

At first it was really dark, but one by one tiny pin points of candlelight began to come on and soon I began to make out that all around me were mirrors. I couldn't believe how many there were. Each mirror reflected a different me like the ones they had in the fun house. I laughed to see myself two feet tall, or fat as Toot. In the mirror directly in front of me I saw myself, the balloon-faced kid. Red and green pom-pom buttons going down the front of my outfit, matching dunce-like hat tipping at a crazy angle. Next to that there were other mirrors with me laughing, crying, screaming.

I was frightened now, no longer trying to figure out how they did those weird effects. I looked for the door, but mirrors blocked my way. I tried to push one aside, but it began to glow blood red and as I looked closer, I saw myself in it. I looked a lot older, but it was definitely me, but in a way it also looked like Charles-in-the-Air-Force. I wore some kind of torn uniform. My face and arms were bandaged. I looked dazed as I staggered out of a burning airplane. My face and arms were cut and I could hear an eerie kind of moaning and could faintly make out blood-covered men struggling across a vast field. "What's happening, what's happening?" I yelled and tried to catch up with one of the men, but he acted like he didnt hear me. I couldn't tell where I was going but I had the feeling something bad was going to happen in that mirror. Lights and explosions began going off, and I shielded my face so I wouldn't have to look. I stood that way a minute, maybe more, listening. I heard rockets and bombs exploding but not *Bald Mountain*.

I gathered up the courage to look into the mirror once again and this time I saw myself eating wedding cake with a nice-looking lady in a bridal gown. She threw her bouquet up in the air and as the flowers touched the floor, the petals became glass and shattered. I cried and looked away. And then I saw myself as a fat, old man with double chins and a big belly. He didn't look like me, but I knew he was me—grown old. His naked eyes stared past me. There were other mirrors farther toward the rear. Each showed a different aspect of my life, one showed me stark naked, in one I looked like a strange animal with fur all around and glowing, beady eyes.

I felt like my skin was jumping off my body when I saw all these reflections of myself. The hair on my scalp was getting ready to get up and leave. I reached out to touch the one mirror that showed me in the clown suit, in order to connect with it. As I did so my reflection reached out too, but with less than perfect timing. That is to say, my pink-faced image in the mirror was moving slower than me! And the hand in the mirror came through to grasp my hand. And the touch of the other me made a sizzling sound that froze my bones.

Then the other me let go, and the candles flickered wildly and there were so many pin-points of light in the room, I couldn't see myself in the mirrors anymore. Then a phosphorescent haze began to envelope the room and everything had a sickly green cast. I spun around. A white figure appeared above my head and blotted out all the mirrors, covered and absorbed my body. I felt hot and steamy inside this—thing. I felt as though I was in a fog; wrapped in moist cotton candy. I struggled, caught in some kind of sticky web, and then I screamed.

"Jason, Jason. Stop that. It's all right." It was Mrs. Tuttle's voice, reassuring and sweet as *Kracker Jacks.* The lights went on and I saw I was standing in the living room with a bunch of mirrors. Some were on dressers, some leaning on chairs. And there on the floor was a white sheet. Mrs. Tuttle held a steaming tea kettle in her hand, passing secret looks to her husband.

"Dear, dear," said Mrs. Tuttle. "It's just a bed sheet. You helped string it up yourself."

I looked up at her, eyes reeling.

"But I saw myself in those mirrors," I cried. "It was me and it wasn't me. It was me in the future. It was terrible."

The Tuttles looked at each other. "Whatever did you see, dear?" Mrs. Tuttle asked.

"You know," I sobbed, "You know."

You took it much too seriously, Dear." They tried to soothe me, "Would you like to come into the kitchen, and join the others for the party? You'll feel better soon as you have some cider."

I didn't stay, I couldn't. I made it to my house in twenty seconds flat.

❏

The next day I spoke to my friends about the Tuttles and they all laughed and talked brave about the worms in the bucket and the sheep eyeballs. They said "That stuff wasn't very scary." But none of the other kids knew what I was talking about when I told them about the room of mirrors, or at least they pretended not to know what I was talking about. I never knew if I was the only one who saw the mirror. Like me, some of them had seen the pictures of Charles. But none of the others expressed the odd feeling of connection I had with him. And now I felt that his life and mine had somehow become interconnected, that his road might be my road. In some inexplicable way, I had received a warning that my childhood was disappearing as fast as a Good Humor truck going around the corner. Then again, I wasnt sure if I had seen myself or Charles in the mirrors of the future, or if both of us were one, but I knew I had seen the far side of a great abyss, a point of no return and I was not yet ready to enter it. And I was glad that for at least a little while, I was Jason-as-I-am, and that I could spend a little more time as a kid.

In early December, the Tuttles told me they were moving to Boulder, Colorado; by the end of January they had packed and gone. "I'll write you one of the cards you sold me," Mrs. T said, but of course she never would.

"You're a damn fine boy," said Mr. T getting into his old black Ford. "We'll be looking out for you," and he drove off waving his left hand, eyes straight ahead.

I watched them disappearing out of my life with a growing sense of sadness, and climbed up onto their front porch and sat down on the swing. Today the swing did not take me to the sky, but remained earth bound. The only thing the Tuttles had left behind was a small, uncarved pumpkin, strangely fresh as it was in October, sitting on the grey floorboards, and I picked it up, turning it idly in my hands. I tried to imagine a face for it, and started carving a Jack-O-Lattern with my Boy Scout pocket knife, the one that could heal or cut or do both at the same time. ❑

Phoebe Frank
© 1996

What Do Aircraft Carriers Do?

In honor of Lieutenant Dan Frank and the aircraft carrier Nimitz

In the middle of the Indian Ocean,
Lime green waves rustle at the hem of the Nimitz.
Immense with its own pleasures and concerns,
It watches jets take off and buzz the tower.

The ship carrier doesn't give a damn.
It does what aircraft carriers do.
Sits heavy in the water and sunbathes when it can,
Shoving the children
Out of the nest to fly against the sun.
Small sparks of jets.

There's a horrible roar when the planes zoom off
Or return to their floating mother.
There are cables on the deck to trip on,
And jet engines that can suck in men
And spit them out again.
Down below the engines rumble,
But the ship doesn't give a damn.

The guys in uniform banter, drink lousy coffee,
Try not to pee or throw up pulling G's.
Relax in the Ready Room,
Not quite ready.

One of those planes hit the drink.
"Not my fault, Man. Not my trip, not my command."
Not quite ready.

Walk the deck.
Look at stars and phosphorescent fish.
Think about the hook, the chase, the lousy coffee.

The ship doesn't give a damn.
It does what aircraft carriers do.
Sits heavy in the water and tries not to worry.

❑

Starched and Ready

MY SHIRT IS WAITING ON THE BED, STARCHED AND STIFF, waiting on the bed for Georgene. It's a shirt my wife picked out last year for my birthday. Pamela doesn't think I've got much taste.

I'm a mid-belt 55, the speed limit in most states. Georgene is coming up to my hotel room, and I'm waiting like water backed up in a garden house, hoping I won't dribble out.

I would like to feel heat once again, the old interior plumbing working, on scientific principles; in order to make water boil, you've got to have a fire. I'd like to feel the way my son, he's a pilot, feels when he's zooming of the aircraft carrier. But instead, I think of how I'll probably pancake on the deck.

I'd like Georgene to tear off my shirt, so I brought an extra one, an old pink one with a frayed collar and an ink stain on the breast pocket that makes it unwearable. My wife Pamela would think it odd if my custom-made shirt was in shreds and the buttons danced off. So, I'm just doing up the old pink.

I'm going into the speckled age now, brown spots all over my skin like small clods of earth. My hands are as big as bricks, just like my father's brick hands, burled as the great redwoods. I could never be like my father. Pamela agrees.

It helps to think about Georgene's body, adrift with mischief, sturdy breasts the shape of ice cream cones, sugar cones, although not as pointed nor as small. I should kiss her when she enters. Yes. "You're beautiful," is good to say, which she actually might be, in a certain light, a careful light.

I bet she's a rosy purple inside, something of a dark cabbage amethyst color, wet and glistening, and that little soldier in there standing up ready to do or be done. All well and good when it's working.

I could get excited if a woman tore off my shirt, but how to ask her? I can't just say, "Would you mind tearing off my shirt? It would mean so much."

"Can't you be creative?" Pamela asks. "Can't you think about anything except business?"

I open the door and invite Georgene in. "You look beautiful," I say,

"Nice shirt " she says as she enters and the light is kind.

❏

Ten Thousand Elephants Spinning Hairnets

Ten thousand elephants were spinning hairnets
From old men's dreams, the kind they used to have
When shoveling snow, the kind
No one takes seriously anymore.

Ten thousand elephants spinning, and at the same time
Twiddling their tuleries.
And I, maladjusted slut that I am,
Dressed only in my bikini line,
Dared nibble on their dildoesque protuberances.
And then with my left arm tied, without so much as a
second thought,
I
Cajoled the nether pachyderm to feret in
My
Sweet potatoes.

It was then I lost my fragility.
I pandered to their lowest elephantine desires as I lay
Splayed upon
The golden tubers.

I must confess I longed to see their dingles dangling
So as to compare, in case they needed a bit of padding.
But there was not a twilerie in a passle.

Odd Rapscalion!
I had hoped to see the tandylions loins, hard pressed
Pissing out their pips in fountains of rapturous dazzle.
Give me an epidermal, you demented pachyderm.
You elephantine toad blender.
But I digress.
I longed to see another pachydermatoid twilerie so
large,
Immense.
Back to the sweet potatoes drenched with rhinocerotic
sperm,
Each one a flacid, fetal pachyderm.
Not that I could describe the odd off-center
quintissitude of my sensations
As the elephantoid fellow left to gather
Other sweet patooties.

❑

Worldwide Elf Restoration Service

THERE IS A WOMAN IN MY NEIGHBORHOOD whom I've never met, who has decaying elf and deer statuary in her front yard. Three dozen or more elves relax among her roses. Every day when I walk or drive by, I see them. They've been there for twenty years, as long as we have lived in our house. The polka dots are fading from the little mens stocking hats, there are tattle-tale grey rings around their collars and their white undercoats are showing.

I want to knock at my neighbor's door, tell her I'm an artist, and offer to repaint her fading gnomes. If you had an exquisite lawn filled with molting elves, wouldn't you want to restore them to their former glory? They need a primer, and vibrant outdoor acryllic enamel colors. But then what if the maid answers and doesn't understand my need to revive these creatures?

It could be magical to work on them right in her garden, in the early morning when the grass is covered with dewy sparkles and the scent of those scarlet roses rides the air.

I could do an elf on spec. But there is a danger. I could easily become obsessed by this art work. A year ago, I got lost in a serious flocking project. Last month I became addicted to gold leaf. After I refinished picture frames, moldings and a carved table, I wanted to gold leaf my computer. It's a sickness.

I went to New Jersey to help my daughter (who was under the weather) and as soon as she mentioned she had a junky chest of drawers that needed refinishing, I started stripping the old paint and sanding it down. I could not be reached for car pooling, cooking or general companionship! I barely surfaced for meals, and I was the one who was supposed to cook them. So there's a part of me that doesn't want to get engulfed by gnomes. But a larger part does.

Phoebe's World-Wide Elf Restoration Service

Maybe I could put a flyer in the woman's mailbox. **Phoebe's World Wide Elf Restoration Service.** That would give the impression that people around the world send me their grimy goblins for repainting. My flyer would read:

Are your elves enervated? Your gargoyles ungainly? **Phoebe's World Wide Elf Restoration Service** will put them right again, restore their luster and their painted smiles. For twenty-five dollars each, your gritty gnomes and other garden gremlins will be cleaned and painted. Guaranteed satisfied customers.

I put in the "World Wide" so it will sound like Calabasas, where I live, is the mecca for elf metamorphosis. I could put the flyer (the only flyer) in her mailbox some evening around midnight. She will hire me for the job, and I will spend my summer in her garden restoring the elves and plaster deer to their former glory.

But wait, what an idea! I could write a letter to the editor of the *Los Angeles Times*. What publicity! She might read the letter and think—oh, I don't know what she'll think. But I'll stop at nothing to get to those elves.

Maybe I could elfnap the little men, (a kind of reverse Snow White). I'd steal one a night for a month or so, repaint it, and place each one back in situ before the next day dawned. She would never know. I can imagine the surprised look on her face when she sees her elves have been brought back to health as if by magic. Of course, I wouldn't earn any money for my troubles that way, but it would be a good deed of the highest nature. The highest *mitzvah* is to do good works anonymously. And an elf *mitzvah* must be among the highest of all.

Or, I could 'nap them all at once and ask for a ransom which would be enough to cover my artistic services. And if she didn't like the way I painted them the first time around, perhaps I could convince her to let me gold leaf them instead. Elfnap! Ransom! Fake flyers! Stealing elves under cover of darkness! What in the world would make a person plot like this? I told you, my art projects are a sickness.

❑

Alphabet Zoop

This zoop can spell.
So play it as it lays,
Arranged in syllables with mostly "a's,"
"Ha be wah tanay," it says.
Or my dish may note
"Tanya cries," if that is what Tanya did.
But if Tanya didn't, it can't say "didn't,"
Lacking "d's."
Or flowing backward from the source
The carrots can be used for "t's"
Except where rutabagas insist
That peas might take the place of "e's".

Vegetables must float
And not stand still,
Since when one tries to drink the zoop
All the stuff falls to the bottom
And the whole puddle is muddled
With things like potatoes
Who have not been informed or assigned a letter.
And who'd like to take over,

As radical tubers are want to do
Since they have underground connections.

Alphabet zoop without "x's,"
Is like a dish of pale strontium 90
Laced with non-irritating soda fiber,
Artificial coloring and ground plaid sofas
For color.

Oh, preternatural zoop preboiled in Ziplock bags.
Dear primordial zoop begotten in an infinite pot,
Goes so well with rolls and butter.
The deep Chompskian structure of zoop
Assures this goop will never stutter.

Well.
At least this zoop can spell.

❑

Norma Spinos

LAST NIGHT A HARD FULL MOON HUNG over the Santa Monica mountains and our nursing station on 2-East began getting quirky indecent calls. As an obstetrical nurse, I can tell you the full moon sends the crazies in here faster than usual. The birthing rooms were all occupied with breaches, false labor, nervous dads, and white lipped moms to be.

I was just going to hide the candy box from Dr. Zarkey. He was a good obstetrician, but had the habit of scooping up any thing edible that wasn't nailed down. The phone rang, and when I turned around, Zarky was heading down 2 East to Melody Mansfields room with his white lab coat pockets bulging. Too late. The candy box was empty. Melody Mansfield was screaming her head off, and I knew that the can of Diet Coke she had ordered, and which now stood on a cart in front of her room, probably wouldn't make it to her. Zarkey had unusually large pockets in his lab coat stuffed with food he pilfered. I had just finished writing all the patients' names on the big white board with a black marker when Brea Fisher's water broke. Just after two that afternoon, Christos Spinos brought in his wife, Norma, presenting with severe back pains.

Mr. Spinos, nervous with a slight facial tick, didn't under-
stand much of what we explained about the birthing proce-
dures. He had only been in the States a short time from Greece
and he spoke no English other than to haltingly say, "Eh, OK."
Norma, who had been born here, spoke for both of them.

His face was the color of weak tea and his body involuntarily
twitched as he accompanied his wife to a birthing room. Shortly
after midnight, for no apparent reason, Norma's pains stopped,
and Dr. Goldman told Christos, who lived only a few minutes
away, to go home and get some rest. The doctor told Christos to
call in the morning for an update. Christos said, "Eh, OK."

Around five AM, 2-East was finally quiet when someone
screamed from the birthing room, and an answering cry soon
heard. Another baby born. It was Zarkey's patient, and I saw
him take a plastic cellophane wrapped sandwich from his lab
coat pocket and munch on it. I was pretty sure he had picked it
up in Brea Fisher's room. I checked Norma on my rounds;
nothing much happening there. "I'll wait a little while to call
Christos," she said. "He's so nervous about all this."

Life slipped into three quarter time. Mansfield delivered a
lovely baby girl with a helmet of black hair, Norma fell asleep
unhappy that her husband hadn't called to see how she was.
Brea was practicing Lamaze breathing. The OB's in the doctor's
lounge dozed. Zarkey entered the lounge and came out a
moment later with a box of uneaten cold pizza slices. I knew he
was going out to his car to empty his pockets and stash his
goods. When he came back he would be ready for refills.

Mercifully all the TVs were off. But at seven-thirty, the first
of the unpleasant calls came. Nurse Wilder picked up the phone
at the front desk, listened and froze.

"What?" Her eye balls stuck out dead center from her head. She blinked. "What?" she said again. Her eyebrows arched abruptly upwards.

"What's the matter," I asked.

"I can't believe this," Wilder crashed down the phone.

"You're white, what happened? What's wrong?"

"Crank call." She drew out a tissue and patted her face. "I can't believe what I heard and I'm not going to repeat it."

Of course we get our share of crank calls, why I even made them when I was in high school. "Do you have Prince Albert in the can?" I would ask the cigarette shop salesman. "Well, let him out of there." That one was a personal highlight for me, but by the look on her face I could tell this call was much more upsetting.

The phone rang again and Wilder made a face before she picked it up. She rolled her eyes upward. This time she listened for a moment, then handed it to me and I heard a man's fierce voice saying, "e-normous penis." I slammed down the phone sharply. It was a little hard to tell, he rolled his R's so and ennunciated every syllable evenly and with great emphasis as though he was trying to make sure we heard him right.

It sure sounded like "enormous penis" to me, I said. Well, L.A. has its share of fruits and nuts, but to call up a maternity ward, and say that, is just plain sick.

We were busy for a few moments with ordinary calls, but every time we picked up the phone, we were cautious. The phone rang again, I answered it and this time the voice was much louder.

"EH-NORMOUS PENIS," he said. Twice.

"Crank ass-hole pervert." I banged down the receiver. I know you're not supposed to talk to the dirty caller, as it gives them satisfaction, but my response gave me satisfaction. Then things calmed down again, so what I did must have worked. Mansfield was sleeping, Norma was unhappy since she hadn't heard from her husband,

Judi Berg checked in, mother of two, ready to deliver her third, the traffic outside on the freeways was picking up. Norma said every time she dialed her home, she got a busy signal, could we check out her phone? I got back to the nursing station about a half hour later, just in time to see Christos collide with Dr. Zarkey who was sneaking a large fruit basket out of Mrs. Mansfield's room. Christos charged down the corridor towards us, skidding on the apples and oranges that rolled across the floor. As Zarkey stooped to pick them up, Nurse Wilder hissed, "you put all that fruit back where you found it."

I was on the desk microphone calling for Dr. Goldman.

Christos looked so mad his hair seemed to be burning. He charged up to the counter and grabbed the microphone.

"I'm so glad you're here," I said hoping to soothe him. "Your wife has been asking for you." In back of him I could see Zarkey putting the oranges back in the basket, and the apples into his lab coat pocket.

If Christos heard, he gave no sign, just jerked the open mike up to his mouth. "EH-NORMOUS PENIS," he bawled, "R's" rolling furiously.

What, Christos our crank caller?

"EH-NORMOUS PENIS," he repeated, voice bouncing off the walls.

Every neck jerked forward, every eye rolled in its sockets. If they didn't hear it the first time, they sure heard it the second. Before one of our hefty attendants could leap on Christos and wrestle the mike away, neck veins pulsating, Christos bleated out one more time, **"EH-NORMOUS PENIS"** and then from a far room down the hall, relieved to hear her husband's voice, Norma Spinos came out of her room and said, "Hi, Honey, why didn't you call?"

❏

That's Not the Way It Works

THE FACT THAT HE HAD KILLED A MAN WAS NOT SO IMPORTANT. But that he killed a man without getting caught haunted him. Then again, he wasn't sure it was his fault. Around 2 AM, Paul Conway had been going at a good clip along Kanan Road, a narrow and dangerous canyon pass cutting from the San Fernando Valley to Malibu. Enormous craggy rocks, several hundred feet high, rose like ghosts over the treacherous winding road, providing spectacular scenery as well as the opportunity for death. Out of nowhere, a convertible came around the hairpin turn heading toward Paul and he applied his brakes sharply. He hit his head on the steering wheel, but the seat belt restraining him prevented serious damage.

The other car, on the outside lane, swerved off the road and over the side of the steep embankment. The convertible top was down and, for a moment before it tumbled madly down the precipe, seemed to hang in the air; the radio blared Bruce Springsteen, and a man screamed.

Paul sat there several moments in shock, not quite clear whose fault it was, or even if they both weren't partially to blame. Dazed and unbelieving, he listened to the victim call for help. There was no shoulder at this section of the hairpin and Paul, still shaking, drove slowly forward to park, then search for the survivor. Suddenly, a giant fireball ripped the night sky and a plume of fire lit up the area. He wasn't sure whether or not he heard screaming any more.

Paul vomited onto his shirt, heaving as if to disgorge the terror, but in that small moment of time, as he drove down the twisted road looking for a place to park, he found he had less and less intention of returning. He imagined that both driver and car had been incinerated. He stopped just long enough to strip off his shirt, hoping that with every mile he drove, the event would seem less and less important. But even as he entered his apartment's garage, the memory settled in, not to be dislodged by any ordinary effort.

Paul had not seen any other cars in either direction just before and after the accident. No one could identify his vehicle; there were no witnesses who could place him at the scene. What would be the point of getting involved? What was done was done. He was single, twenty-nine years old with a good job as the manager of an independently owned, sophisticated bookstore, and he was not prepared to go out of his way for a dead man. The best course was to do nothing.

❑

The ship's bells rang six times every noon just before lunch. It was a loud, melodic sound broadcast over the vessel's public address system. The passengers' mouths watered, like those of well trained Pavlovian subjects, at the sound of the dinner gong, and everyone lined up for another bountiful meal, even though the last vestiges of their hunger had long been extinguished.

Paul sat on a blue-cushioned lounge chair on the promenade deck, reading his guide book. The *Artemis Opal* would anchor off Devil's Island tomorrow for an early morning tour. In 1854 the French had established the infamous prison on the Salvation Islands, sometimes translated from the French as the Safety Islands. Three specks of land, ten miles off the coast of French Guiana, make up the Salvation Islands *(Ile du Salut):* Il Royale, St. Joseph, and Devil's Island. Salvation or safety, he could use them both. The main installation of the penal colony was a hostile, escape-proof place where Albert Dreyfuss and Henri Charreire, better known as Papillon, had been imprisoned.

Paul put the guide book down, trying to imagine what life had been like for Papillon, and shivered. He wished he had brought a sweater to wear at lunch. Though it was a humid 80 degrees in the sun, with a slight wind blowing, he felt chilled. He had a headache hammering beneath the scar on his right temple, still visible a year after what he preferred to think of as the "incident," and it corrupted the perfection of his face.

His nose was straight with a slight upward tilt to the nostrils, and his square face and sharply defined chin gave a certain intractability to his countenance. His face was ringed by wavy blonde hair, which fell across his forehead, partially hiding the angry scar. He walked with his head tilted slightly downward so as to avoid eye contact with the other travelers.

Paul's work had suffered since the accident. He had driven straight home without trying to help or report the accident and locked himself in his book-lined living room, there to seek the comfort of serious writers like Henry James, DeMaupassant, and Poe. An eclectic assortment of melancholy works, that spoke directly to him. He stayed up all night reading because he was too anxious to sleep. The following morning, a short paragraph on page two of the *Los Angeles Times* reported that the victim was a teenage boy on the way home from his high school prom. Thank God they were not looking for Paul. The cockatiel in its cage did not look at him differently; he was not smote by lightning. Everything familiar remained in place.

As the months went by, Paul had buried the details of that night in the deepest, most inaccessible part of his memory, and the cries, the explosion and the Springsteen song settled like an old wrecked ship to the floor of his consciousness. But the beleaguered vessel, as it sank further and further down into the silt of forgetfulness, still sent out erratic bubbles of pain that every so often, threatened to break on the surface of his life.

Since the accident, his face had taken on a pale and gaunt appearance. His small circle of friends and colleagues thought he looked tired and depressed, and advised a long vacation.

So Paul, being a rather literary young man, which is not so much in fashion nowadays, signed up for the cruise solely because it would make a short morning stop at Devils Island. He had read the story of Papillon, had seen the movie with Steve McQueen and Dustin Hoffman, and somehow figured that at this place of forced labor and no return, he would find expiation. Not that he could have explained his idea, for it was chained to his sunken memories. Somehow, he would live out the life of the damned, throw himself in an abandoned cell of the former penal colony and allow all that festered inside to escape, like pus from a boil.

He figured his atonement might last the better part of a day, that he would return at six bells to the comfort of his ship and be done with suffering. He knew that his plan was somewhat romantic; quixotic even, and thus the idea was even more ideally suited to his nature. But in making this unspoken bargain with himself, he did not realize that his inner life was a strong keeper of the faith, and that it would not let him get off so easily.

And so having declared to himself his intention, Paul boarded the *Artemis Opal* in Manaus, Brazil, and did not leave the ship until he reached Devil's Island.

❏

The Wyley-Smythes, two of Paul's table mates, noticed him sitting in a deck chair and invited him to come along for lunch.

Table seating was a bit like poker; he was dealt the Wyley-Smythes (an octogenarian pair on their twenty-ninth cruise), the Dancing Couple, the Gassets; Mr. Perry Pringle (the Man with the Plastic Leg), and Ms. Constance Ferand, a young woman given to wearing as little as possible.

The Dancing Couple taught the Cha-Cha-Cha. They kept the passengers happy with lessons every afternoon at three, just before tea time. They looked so much alike to Paul that he had a hard time telling one from another. The lady part of the Dancing Couple wore no make up or jewelry; the gentleman partner was smooth shaven and slight. They were his first truly androgynous set of matched human beings who finished each others sentences and dinners.

Paul Conway got along with everybody by keeping his mouth shut, withdrawing more and more into himself. Soon the table ignored him (all except Ms. Ferand, who was intrigued by his noncommunication). They treated him with little more interest than they did their linen napkins.

He appeared only at dinner and listened to the reports the Dancing Couple delivered on the day's activities. Even though he hated their endless prattle, the couple provided enough information to make Paul feel content not to have suffered the unpleasant inconvenience of trekking back and forth ashore.

When at lunch one day, Mrs. Wyley-Smythe remarked that such a handsome young man, such a nice quiet young man, needed the companionship of a sweet young lady, Ms. Ferand pouted. Then the elder woman, with no encouragement from anyone, passed a picture around of their daughter, Lydia, a young woman with a port wine stain on her sallow cheek. A kind of a match-mate, Paul thought, to his own angry scar.

After lunch that day, the Man with the Plastic Leg propelled Ms. Ferand across the dance floor with a grim smile, and won the dance contest much to the consternation of the Dancing Couple, who had an energetic, if not graceful, approach to rhythm. Paul watched the show without interest and listened to the Wyle-Smythes carping that Pringle might have had the courtesy not to dance in shorts, parading around his cream-colored plastic appendage, with the two dark bolts on either side of his knee and an elastic bandage riding above it.

When the sun set, Paul took a quiet walk on the promenade deck trailed by Constance Ferand. She had the habit of falling for men outrageously bad for her, and had already succumbed to Paul, who consistently ignored her.

❑

Paul decided to go to sleep early the night before they landed on Devil's Island. Because the morning tour was so brief, he wanted to go out on the early tender with the ships setup staff. The tender was a small boat used by the cruise line to ferry people ashore. The more he read about Papillon's incarceration, the more he looked forward to seeing the island which had once served as a prison for France's most dangerous criminals. They had been used as forced labor to drain the swamps and haul the stones for the roads. It sounded like one of the places on earth where Hell was external, and he could do penance in steaming dampness. He would sink into heat he could really feel, bake in it, broil in it, and have his soul roasted. But a voice in his head asked, who was he kidding? Did he really think that touring this miserable place was a way to suffer enough to bring salvation?

❑

He kept the air conditioning off when he went to sleep that night, and even so, when he got into bed it was like sliding in between two slabs of ice. He piled the covers on top of him and marveled at how he could be so near the equator freezing to death.

❑

In the morning, he rose early, put on his favorite pine-scented after-shave lotion. Determined to explore the island before the other 1,200 passengers got there, Paul persuaded the tour office to let him go with the setup team at 7:30 AM. On shore, the cruise director and his staff set big blue and white umbrellas to shade the huge metal containers of chilled orange juice to be served to the thirsty tourists.

As soon as he was off the tender, Paul took his map and guide book and headed for the low road that led to the Children's Cemetery. They were the offspring of the prison staff who had succumbed to a variety of diseases.

No prisoners were buried anywhere on this island. They had not been eaten by worms, but by sharks. Their bodies were placed in a reusable casket, and dumped through the bottom of it a mile or so out to sea. The sharks ripped apart their bodies as easily as if they were communion wafers.

At first the heat seemed comforting, and Paul was glad to feel his body slowly warming up. But as time went by, the heat became oppressive and suffocating, sliding down the surface of his skin, forming rivulets of sweat that hugged his body like a limp overcoat.

The jungle vegetation spread like a tangled mass of spaghetti on either side of the cobblestoned incline, insinuated itself into the crumbling walls of the buildings, the grave markers, and in the tiny spaces between the rocks. Small fruit, the shape of miniature green apples, fell from some of the trees and squished beneath Paul's feet. The guidebook said they were poisonous.

Palm fronds, trees, hanging vines, brush, leafy plants fought for space with each other, and the heat grew more intense. Pallid, grey coconuts lay scattered about in various degrees of decay. Some had cracked, exposing a hard fleshy surface; some were blackened or scorched by errant fires, and they vaguely reminded him of shrunken human heads.

And all around a mournful, silent presence of plants decaying, returning to their past and future. Even the most upright tree would someday kneel to its fate. But there was something else that hung in the air along with the deep green scent oozing from the earth. Paul experienced it as a flickering from the treetops, a shadow that passed between him and the sun and was gone before he could glimpse it. All he saw, as he frequently stopped to mop his brow, were the tops of the trees, enormous, cone-shaped termite mounds hanging down from them like monstrous, cancerous growths. A tangle of aerial vines swarmed through the forest, sweetly sucking out the life from their hosts.

Through the trees off to his left, he could see water, hear it lapping against the jagged rocks. He could see the first tourist tender docking at the pier. Suddenly, in front of him, a building appeared that was not in the guide book. It was no larger than a tool shed, with thick concrete walls. He went up to it to investigate. A heavy wooden door hung open on broken hinges. Paul tried to open the door all the way, but it would not move.

He guessed this must have been an isolation cell and shuddered, making himself enter the tiny cubicle to better imagine the suffering of its former prisoners. This was what he had come for. He half thought to sit down on a ragged mattress that lay on a dirt floor. The darkness dazed him for a moment, but as his eyes became used to the gloom he was startled to see a man in ragged prison clothes sitting on the mattress. He stared at Paul with tired, accusing eyes. The smell of human feces filled the squalid, windowless room.

"*Entre, Monsieur,*" said the man in a gravelly voice.

The hackles on Paul's neck rose; goose bumps appeared on his arms as the man, shackled to the wall by leg irons, beckoned him in. For a moment he was frozen to the spot, incapable of moving. A foul stench issued from the man's mouth with each unintelligible word he uttered. For a moment Paul was rooted to the spot; the image had a strange shimmering quality, as though it was composed of shafts of darkness and light that alternated with each other, giving the whole scene a kind of stroboscopic effect. Willing himself to move, Paul took a step back into the sunlight, so strong it seemed to bite him when he stepped outside.

He found himself standing outside the hut, shaking in the glare of the jungle sun that poured like hot molten steel onto everything around him. He closed his eyes as if to reassure himself that he had not seen the vision. When he opened his eyes again, the heavy door was closed fast upon its broken hinges.

Nausea leaped to his throat, and his whole body shook. In a panic, he became disoriented, wanted to run back to the ship, but found himself, instead, running forward toward the Children's Cemetery. He entered the small, square enclosure through the open gate of a wrought iron fence.

It was 9:00AM. His fellow passengers began to make their way toward the graveyard, and the sight of them, twittering like brightly colored birds, reassured him. The Dancing Couple was in the lead, followed by the Man with the Plastic Leg. Unfamiliar faces trailed them; Paul marveled how people he had never noticed on the cruise before, kept appearing. The tourists walked unusually slowly. Like Zeno's arrow, they kept climbing the path toward him without ever reaching him.

He tried to pull himself together, but his hands were still trembling. A slight breeze rustled and once more he sensed, but did not see, a shape flickering, this time around the tree trunks.

He turned and saw a young woman who had entered just in back of him.

Her skin was framed by long dark hair pulled tightly into an upsweep with wispy ends hanging down her neck. Her rich, full mouth was a delicate pinkish hue, her dark eyes set against long, full lashes. She wore a flashing crystal necklace and an ankle length lace dress the color of faded, pressed flowers. A diaphaneous white veil tied loosely around her neck, floated in back of her as she glided effortlessly forward.

Since the other passengers had not yet reached this spot, Paul figured she must be part of the twenty or so set-up staff who had come on the tender with him, although he did not remember seeing her on the boat. He walked inside through the open black wrought iron gate, prepared to ignore the young woman, but she came to stand directly in front of him.

"A pity, isn't it, poor child," she said to him an easy conversational way, as though she knew him, and pointed to a gravestone. The marble edges had been eaten away leaving only a pale graven epitaph:

DENISE COURTALON

28 JUIN - 12 OCTOBRE, 1905

"*Pouvre petite,*" she said and laid the flowers on the untidy grave.

Paul looked at the headstone and those of its nearest companions and noticed how the monuments were crumbling. Small plants were sprouting from within the stones. Here in the jungle, the forest was eating the dead.

"Poor child," the woman repeated, and sighed, then turned to him and spoke in a heavily accented English, "Her life was short and not very sweet. Are you French?"

"No, American," he said, wondering how he had not noticed a woman so ravishing on board the ship. "Why?"

She smiled pleasantly and opened a parasol with a dainty gesture.

"You remind me of someone," she said, her English tipped with a rolling French accent. She inspected him closely, the way one looks at an animal in the pound, hoping to find the familiar characteristics of a loved pet.

"You remind me of Louis Daumier," she said, turning to walk on to another monument.

He followed her. "I'm Paul Conway." He didn't know what else to say.

"Louis Daumier — he was my fiance. You look much like him. He was tall, like you. Blue eyes like you. But you, you smell of pine trees, and he, how shall I say it — of salt water and swamp."

She reached out as though to touch Paul's face but he felt only the slightest movement of air between them, like the delicate brush of a butterfly's wing.

"I'm Gisette," she said as she fingered her necklace. Behind the young woman he could see the Dancing Couple and the other brightly attired tourists beginning to enter the tiny cemetery, moving slowly as though their legs were attached to heavy weights.

The angelic look of the woman intrigued him, awakening a feeling he had never expected; something beyond chemical attraction, though certainly that was there. Intuitively, he felt that a woman who had been engaged to a criminal must have a heart big enough to accept him and his story.

He fancied that she belonged to another era; one of bustles and herringbone corsets and upswept hair. Although she was not dressed in shorts like most of the women on the tour, Gisette's clothes were not entirely out of place either. Her dress looked typical of the kind of attire that young women of his acquaintance often bought in trendy used clothing stores. The English she used was halting and grammatically correct, as though she had learned it at school but not used it much in real life. And Paul had to admit that her language, looks and dress had a profound effect on him.

Miss Ferand, Paul's comely pursuer, walked in through the gate and looked for a moment as though she were going to come over to talk, but instead she ignored him and turned away.

It was 11:15, almost time to go back to the shore where the tender would be starting to load passengers. Suddenly, he wanted nothing more than to run down the path to grab the boat back to the *Artemis Opal.*

But he couldn't move. Some peculiar force bound him to the spot, had in fact caused his gaze as well as his footsteps to move swiftly in Gisette's direction instead. He noted with a start that she had left his side, gone through the gate and was making her way up a hill. He ran to catch up with her.

Her face seemed to have some kind of shiny white glaze, and her obsidian eyes were veiled by thick lashes. She was as somber as the shadows surrounding her. The necklace flashed, and it seemed for a moment not to be crystal at all, but formed by the tears that trickled down her face.

"They are ringing the bells for him," she said, dabbing at her eyes prettily. "*Alors,* we must not be late."

"Where are you going? What do you hear?" Paul heard nothing but insects buzzing.

"We mustn't be late," she said again, as though he should know what she was talking about.

She turned and left the cemetery, walking up the slight hill toward the lighthouse. "They ring the bells when there are burials at sea." He fell in step beside her.

The island was filled with tourists now, strolling more languidly than before, not seeming to have made any progress at all toward their destination. Two elderly women, one with silver, the other with bright apricot hair looked ready to collapse as they sipped water from large plastic bottles of *Pierval.* The slower the tourists walked, the faster the dark-haired woman ran; Paul gasped to keep up with her.

Gisette did not look back, but still he felt her calling him in some strange, silent way and he followed.

"Today they'll bury Louis. Tomorrow someone else."

"Today?" he asked and wondered how that could be. She was talking about a man who had died more than a hundred years ago. How could it be possible they were burying him today? Paul had to walk fast to keep up with her. "I don't understand what happened to Louis and the other man," he said.

"They were both criminals. Louis had been imprisoned here for just a few months when he realized he would never be able to last out his sentence. The filth, the heat, the bugs, the disease. Monsieur, you cannot know what it was like. I came from France, hired on as a nurse. Louis told me he had to escape. You can't leave Devil's Island in anything but a boat or a box. He bribed one of the guards, Petrial, to get a boat. Louis gave him the last of the money he had hidden, and one night decided to chance it. He was afraid of the shark-infested water, or of being recaptured and thrown into solitary. The other man I don't know much about. A day later he made the same escape attempt, stole what he thought was the rowboat used to transport the coffins. But instead, it was a different one, old and leaking and when the boat sank, the sharks got him."

The woman stood close to Paul, her pale lips and face dappled with shadows. "Louis did not even reach the boat before they recaptured him. The guard liked to play a little game on the unsuspecting. He would show the prisoner the boat they used for burials at sea, then make a switch and the prisoner buys a boat that won't even float. Petrial had sold that boat many times over. The prisoners were always picked up before they could set foot in the boat. And, as I've told you, even if a prisoner made it, the boat inevitably sank. Another dinner for the sharks. Hear the bells, they are ringing now." Gisette twirled the parasol on her shoulder.

Paul heard nothing and noticed with a start that though trees and buildings cast shadows across the road, the woman and parasol did not.

"Louis was picked up by the search party. They threw him into solitary, that little hut right by the Children's Cemetery, and he died. We were to have been married."

Her voice trembled. "Do you want to see the boat they haul the coffins in? They've modernized it; today its a motor boat. You can't get off the island without a boat."

He said yes, he did want to see it. A curiosity, a longing, drove him to view for himself the other man's destiny, as if to reassure himself that it would not be his own. Even if he had not completed his penance, even if, in all candor, he had not even started it, he had a wonderful cruise ship waiting to take him away, not a ridiculous motor boat. The apparition of the prisoner in the isolation hut, the imponderable heat, Gisette and the things she told him made him feel that the sentence he had imposed on himself was too harsh, and he was willing to relinquish it. When he got home after the trip, he would go to the police. He had done nothing more than not report an accident. They would understand. There were worse crimes committed every day. His offense was slight by comparison. Everything would work out all right.

Gisette turned away from him, left the path and plunged into the jungle forest. She darted through the trees and underbrush with ease while Paul followed dumbly after. Branches tore at his skin, scratched his bare arms. He tumbled over a gnarled, exposed root that grasped the earth as though it were trying to strangle it. Paul fell forward, hitting his head on a rock, reopening the old wound on his forehead. Dirt and ants clung to the blood that trickled down from the gash, and he wiped them off with the back of his hand. The sharp boulders didn't deter

Gisette, although Paul stumbled at every turn. The verdant green was no longer a hovering aroma, but the stench of decomposing vegetation.

The heat of the sun seemed to have worked itself into his brain; a thick golden light suffused everything. All the colors of the jungle were lightened. The deep green of the trees and vines became a brilliant yellow chartreuse, dark shadows melted into the sunshine, the water below him sparkled like quartz crystals, and the girl who danced before him, just out of reach, seemed more a beacon of light than a woman.

He looked up. The canopy of the forest was a hundred feet high, standing straight and tall as spears, the tops of which seemed to merge in the diaphanous cloud cover. Epiphytes, air plants, clung to the vegetation. Leaves massed on the forest floor harboring small insects and beetles. Roots ran along the soil like giant twisted wires, a variety of plants sprouting from them, and all were covered by a light dusting of the silky fibres of the kapok tree. Here and there silk trees with their blood red flowers tossed their heads skyward, secure above their trunks, which were covered with thorns all around. The forest was a profusion of Brazil nut, kapok, mahogany and rosewood trees; sunlight fell between their branches, and butterflies fluttered through every available space, drifting like golden banners.

He got up, wiped the sweat off his forehead with a handkerchief, but found it was not perspiration, but blood.

The strange thing about the woman was that she was able to stay ahead of him, occasionally glancing back to see if he would follow, always keeping just out of reach. Yet he could see everything about her clearly, the wisps of hair damply curling on her neck, the pale dress that she wore seemed to be woven of some type of gossamer material. She had an extraordinary effect on him, pulling him toward her, as though he were a fish caught on an invisible line and she was reeling him in, flapping and struggling for air.

Even as he ran he engaged himself in dialogue. This was crazy, this was irrational. What on earth could this woman possibly mean to him? Why was she running away from him? Was she a Lorelei, a siren who lured sailors to their deaths? That was ridiculous! She had said very little, surely not sung. And furthermore he was already on the island, not a sailor at sea.

Thinking of the sea, however, reminded him to look at his watch. Eleven-thirty. Just about time to go.

But before he left, he wanted to tell her everything he had been through since the accident. She above all people could understand him. God knows what crimes Louis had committed, surely much worse than Paul's. He had never planned to kill anyone, it was just that he had not gone for help. Looking at it this way, he told himself, it was not so much of a crime, after all.

He wanted to suffer in small manageable bits, to indulge his sorrow. He was unfairly doomed, but the fate he selected was relentless Her heart would have pity, he knew it. He was sorry, he was sorry, he needed to tell someone he was sorry. He needed to go over every detail of that suppressed moment, needed to explain to the woman how it really hadn't been his fault. He was just an unlucky bystander; there was nothing he could have done, nothing that would have helped. He wanted to vomit up the ugly pain, bring it up through the dark tunnels of his mind, expose everything to the unrelenting sun, disgorge his memory upon the grass and offer it up to her so she would understand and comfort him. This was the siren song her smile promised. Forgiveness —and then he could have forgetfulness at last.

They reached a spot on the rocky escarpment where a tiny vessel lay moored. He clambered after her, as she jumped effortlessly from rock to rock. He could see the blue sea, the froth of waves breaking on the craggy shore, and he was struck by both the reality and the unreality of the scene. What was real was the way his body felt, winded and perspiring from the exertion in the unfamiliar damp and draining heat. The rocks upon which he now stood, the water hissing on the shore, sounded like a pot beginning to boil.

The unreal part was how caught up he was in the pursuit of Gisette. He had met her only moments ago, but from the first, something within her promised the end to his pain. She was certainly no more striking than the comely Constance Ferand, for example, but Constance did not have the depth to understand him.

"The bells are still ringing," she said stopping on the rocks that lined the shore.

He heard nothing.

"See out there," she pointed to a lone rowboat in the water. He scanned the horizon and made out a row boat with two men and a long box.

"That's Louis out there," she said. Then Paul heard the bells ringing, a sound so cavernous and deep that it reverberated in his heart. A coffin was lifted over the keel with a dark package ready to be delivered to the deep. A body slid out. Fierce blades in the water circled momentarily, then disappeared.

"The sharks have been salivating to the bell for generations now. The bells bring them, the blood excites them. Why, even if years go by without a burial, the sharks remember what the ringing of the bells means. They pass it on one to another. They don't forget."

Gisette bent down and pulled back shrubbery branches to reveal a fairly modern, well kept looking motor boat tied to it. The boat looked freshly painted, surprisingly seaworthy. Oars were in the oar locks, supplies and a bailing cup under the broken front seat.

"I've got to get something off my chest," he said, testing to see how she would respond.

"Yes," she said. "You seem like a man possessed. You seem very unhappy about something."

Paul took her remarks as an invitation to speak and rapidly described what had happened to him and why he had come here.

She listened intently, but when he came to the end of his story did not offer him the solace he sought, but spoke about herself, instead.

"I need to tell you about my past, too," she said. "I left out certain parts."

Paul hadn't much patience for hers. He could see the beach from where he stood. The last tender was loading up. He had to leave.

"I didn't tell you exactly what happened to Louis. You see, I loved him so much, more than I could possibly say. I knew that even if he got in the boat, he could not escape in it. Everyone except the prisoners knew it was not seaworthy and a convict had no chance against the sharks. It was a big joke among the staff. But the idea he might die in such a terrible way was too much. Petrial thought, when I told him about Louis' plan to escape, I was doing it for the reward. I did it to save his life, *mon cher*. I was pregnant with his child, Denise. Remember the little grave you saw at the cemetery? Her father was caught, they took him to the isolation hut and beat him to a pulp. He never regained consciousness. I have been on this island ever since, not being able to rest. That's the burden I'm carrying and I see no way of putting it down."

Paul took a step toward Gisette. He remembered the grave marker, the vision he had seen in the filthy room.

"You aren't the only one being punished, but you made the mistake of thinking that I could grant you salvation."

He nodded dumbly.

"You thought you could get out of the bargain you made with yourself. Well, I hate to tell you, but that's not the way it works."

He was close enough to inhale her perfume: something ginger mixed with mothballs, something ripe and not used, something yearning and forgotten. And then, just for a moment, as he drew nearer, the horrible, fetid odor of rotting flesh. Then all was sweet again.

Paul felt fear grab him by the neck, and he took a step back. Gisette looked cool and dry, while he was sweating profusely, his face bathed in moisture. He reached for her hand, and when he grasped it, it felt as though all the bones beneath her skin had melted. The flesh seemed to have no more substance than steam on a mirror and he dropped it as if it had burned through him.

"I'm glad you've decided to stay," the woman said and reached out to touch his arm.

"Decided?" and he was suddenly aware that as he looked out at the tiny harbor, the blue and white umbrellas the *Artemis Opal* crew had set up were gone. The orange juice tanks and paper cups were gone. There were no people waiting to go back to the ship. Then he saw that the last tender had already left. The ship, the ship! He looked about desperately, fearing that it, too, had departed, but it was still there hovering several miles away. A feeling of nausea rose in his stomach, leaping for his throat. He had to escape from the island.

Gisette said nothing. He looked at his watch. The *Artemis Opal* was scheduled to leave at noon and it was 11:45.

He felt her hand tighten on his arm. Gisette's grasp had the force of a vise. Her red tipped fingers felt like giant talons.

"You must stay," she said, more as a command than an invitation.

He felt like a butterfly pinned through the heart as he tried to break her hold. The water near their feet frothed and churned; drops of rain began to fall from a cloudless sky, making the slimy rocks they were standing on even more slippery.

He looked at her, half expecting her to have changed into a ghoulish specter. But her beauty was simply more dazzling than ever. He imagined living on the island with her forever.

The hum of insects was incessant. He saw himself splitting off from his body, leaving Gisette. Part of him escaping in the motor boat, part of him on the shore watching. The stench arose again. The winds whirled.

Eleven forty-six! Salvation could wait, but the ship wouldn't.

He tried to step away from her, to break her hold, but the ethereal being seemed to weigh five hundred pounds. He pulled backward; her arm seemed longer than a human being's could possibly be. He was pulling her toward the water. Now he read fear in her face. He was in a tug of war between Gisette and the sea. He was desperate to get away, and he yanked his arm sharply. A searing pain shot through his arm as if it had been pierced by an ice tongs. His pulse raced; pain shot through him.

The young woman, lovely as ever, leaned against the palm growing out from the rocks at an awkward angle. Her hand, impossibly long, clung to him as he tried to wriggle out of her grasp.

"Paul," she called. He stepped further out on the wicked-looking rocks, stumbling toward the boat.

"Yes, of course," he thought "I'll use the motor boat to catch up with the ship." It was the only course of action.

He was at the boat in a few steps and climbed aboard. The tender had met the ship and was being hauled up to its mooring place. If the coxswain on the tender didn't see Paul, the Officer of the Watch on the cruise ship would. There was nothing to worry about, he could make it easily. He untied the motor boat and pulled on the engine.

Impossibly, her arm reached out and found his boat, blood flecked talons hovered, gouging its keel, leaving deep scratches on its surface. Then he felt her grip on his arm once more. His left arm felt as though it was being torn from his body. His forehead itched beneath the open cut. A little blood still oozed.

He headed toward the ship, motor putting nicely. He took off his shirt and waved it, but no one looked his way or heard him.

Paul's heart beat wildly. No sign of the woman on the distant shore. He felt a sense of relief. The whole thing, his encounter with her, all some kind of strange delusion.

But now he felt water slowly seeping into his canvas shoes. The boat suddenly looked older than it had before, and water was spurting in. Even if he could bail the boat, he would lose the ship. He grabbed the oars and threw himself into a frenzy of paddling. The boat responded. He'd make it.

"Help," he called, but knew that although he was not that far away, his voice could not reach the ship. Surely someone would see his little boat and everything would work.

Suddenly Gisette was sitting in the bow on the broken seat in front of him, her hair strewn with green vines and seaweed, hands sedately folded in her lap.

"You'll stay, won't you?" she smiled, and he noticed her teeth had a yellow cast. The bottom of the boat was slowly filling with water. He threw water from the bailing cup at her and the drops of water formed a cloud of vapor around her. Each tiny droplet sparkled like the sun, and in that instant she was gone.

It was almost noon. He saw fins above the water, coming closer. There was a good chance the sharks were far enough away or were too well fed to bother with him. The boat slowly filled with water as he rowed. The oars grew more and more difficult to maneuver, the boat was almost under water.

He had no choice but to swim for the ship. All the passengers were on board by now. He swam away from his motor boat with deep regret as it began to sink. He moved forward and noted some place from the observational part of his brain that three shark blades were trailing him.

A most peculiar feeling engulfed him. He longed to see Miss Ferand, to walk with her in the sunlight. Throughout the whole trip he had viewed his fellow passengers with contempt: their games doltish, their meals ostentatious and excessive. But now, suddenly, he thought he had never known a livelier, more charming group of people. The thought of eating three meals a day with them was incredibly gratifying; marching on the grey planked promenade deck with such companions, marvelously invigorating. The Wyley-Smythes were cheerfully paternal, Mr. Pringle courageous for dancing in his shorts, and Ms. Ferand's body invited exploration. He imagined the orchestra playing, the sound of bubbly pouring, the Dancing Couple dancing. What a beautiful scene and he had thrown it all away.

God damn it, why don't they see me? he thought as he swam, I'm not that far away from the ship. Why don't they look this way? The fins were much closer now. Across the river, he could see giant trees that formed the shapes of mastodons, lumbering along under a lacy canopy. Salt water licked the inside of his mouth as though to hint of what was inevitably coming. A certain pungent odor entered his nostrils, something that smelled like dark green parsley, water and decay. It was a deep smell. It was the scent of fear that Paul inhaled, and he felt it sink to the bottom of his soul.

❑

A moment or two before twelve, the Wyley-Smythes looked out over the water toward Devil's Island and noticed an empty, grey, weathered rowboat with a broken front seat drifting toward them.

"What in the world is that little bucket doing out here? Why, its floating almost completely under water. How odd." Mr. Wyley-Smythe remarked to his wife as he carefully helped her adjust a lace shawl around her shoulders.

"I'm sure I don't know, dear," his wife answered, her mind on other things.

Then, exactly at noon, the Captain of the Watch rang the ship's bells and the Wyley-Smythes along with the Dancing Couple, the Man With the Plastic Leg, Constance Ferand, and all the other passengers, hurried into the gourmet luncheon buffet, even though they were not really that hungry.

❑

How Was the Food on the Cruise?

We ate and ate and ate and ate,
Until they had to ship us home by freight.

❑

Table Mates

I prayed to the spirit of Wolfgang Puck,
Patron saint of the diner,
To get us two non-smoking seats
At a table for eight
For the second sitting.
A table where the calorie conscious
Did not divulge their cholesterol counts
Or trade recipes for
Tofu teriyaki.

I prayed that if our tablemates
Were singular
Ladies of a certain age,
With sensible shoes and nonsensical hopes,
They would not discuss their last trips
On the Queen, or the Royal Caribbean.

I prayed the maitre d' would know
What we meant when he
Unbent the ten spot we slipped him when we
Requested to be with people "like us."
But when he did as we asked, and led us to tea,
We found that people like us
Were not what we wanted to be.

Intourists are Out

She counted us in two straight lines,
She counted us so many times.
She counted us in Pushkin Palace,
She counted us, the guide
   With malice.

The Hermitage was just the same,
Another brutal numbers game.
On the city tour with resurrected
   Churches,
We fled her gaze to make our purchase.
And on and off the bus she'd count
We dared not have the wrong amount.

"Please follow me and do not tarry,
I must count all cameras you will carry."
And though the old regime is out,
The tourist trade's a sorry lot.
If you miss your bus,
   Your guide is shot.

❑

Funny, You Don't Look Fluish

I have a bug up my nose and
I suppose
It's influenza
A or B.
Whatever its name,
I'm still in great pain.
It could be the Swine flu or
The Hong Kong strain.

I've got headache and fever.
I've starved it and fed it,
And though I regret it
The doc gave me a shot but
I can't seem to shed it.
I'm sneezing a lot,
What a bad cold I've got.

My eyes are red,
And some squirrel is gnawing
On steel drums in my head.
Whatever it is, there is no cure,
I'm simply suffering from
Flu de jour.

194

Phoebe Frank
© 1996

Ascending Angel

I WAS ON THE INTERNET, teaching an on-line computer course sponsored by the University of Alaska, when someone rang the front doorbell. I wheeled myself to the door and reached up to open the special hand lock I had installed. I was in a grumpy mood.

"Hi, I'm Rachel Peace," she said and put down two huge suitcases.

I was taken aback for a moment. She was better looking than I had expected. She had answered my ad in *AlaskaMen*, a singles' magazine devoted to, well, advertising Alaskan men. We had been corresponding for about a year and suddenly, here she was, taking me up on my invitation to come down from Anchorage and visit. She had moved here two years ago from New Yawk. I told her about being in the chair, and though she looked at me carefully, her eyes made no comment on my condition.

I'm used to it — the look of questioning and pain that creeps into the face of someone I've just met, that even hangs around the mouths of people I know well.

Rachel bent down to give me a cursory kiss, and the smell of roses wafted around her.

"Bo Bungadeen, I'm glad to meet you after all these months."

"Come in," I said. "I can't believe you're here. Would you like to look around?"

She chatted all the while she looked. She took after her grandfather, she said as she thumped about. Grampa's chief claim to greatness was his ability to spend money like it was greased with oil. Her great grandfather came here during the Gold Rush and died when his horse dropped dead from starvation, and fell over the rim of Dead Horse Gulch. Down they went to the bottom of the crevasse along with hundreds of others, who instead of tasting the golden life, died with the flavor of dirt in their mouths.

She made a cursory inspection of the so-called "mother-in-law room" she was going to stay in while we got acquainted. It had a small kitchen with a microwave, oven, and a refrigerator.

"I see you've got a baleen basket made from a whale's mouth," she said, letting me know me that she knew baleen when she saw it.

Chechaquos usually think these baskets are woven out of old rubber tires. Newcomers to Alaska don't know what they're looking at most times.

She looked around the living room, past my computer sitting on the dining room sideboard, past the big glass jugs of beer I was brewing in the living room. She glanced at the old chessboard sitting on a coffee table, my juggling balls parked on the window sill and noticed the flow of bills spread out like cream on the roll top desk.

She checked the balcony outside. "That jacuzzi work?"

"Sure. Wait 'til you go skinny dipping in minus zero weather."

She came inside, pointed to the chessboard. "You're missing a king."

"Don't need a king to play chess," I said.

"You need the king to win, though, Mr. Bungadeen."

Chechaquos usually can't pronounce my name right, and she couldn't either. "No mind. Bo will do," I said. She had a point, but I wasn't there to argue it.

She took one look at the balcony's view of Mt. McKinley in the distance peeking out through oyster-colored clouds, and sighed. Her red hair was piled up on top of her head in a ferocious mess that threatened to tumble down any moment, and she blew a wisp out of her eyes. Her lipstick and nail polish were red as the stripes on the American flag. Her voice was husky with hidden notes of sleep in it. I didn't know she'd be so uppity, breathing life into all my dead spaces.

I offered her a drink and she sat down on the sofa.

"You look a little different than your picture," she said.

It was true that I didn't look exactly like the old photograph of me that I had sent her. It had been taken five years ago when I had more hair and, a pretty well-developed upper body and a keep your sympathy to yourself attitude. I'm still not so bad for a thirty-five-year old guy in a permanent sitting position.

My mom tells everybody, "He could have been a movie star." And then her eyes glaze over, and everyone knows that the rest of the sentence was, "If he wasn't in a wheelchair." I wouldn't have minded being a movie star but there's not much call for one in Fairbanks. As for being chair-bound, I've been this way since childhood and I don't want to talk about it.

Rachel sighed. "I didn't tell you when we began corresponding that I was engaged." She sat down on the couch.

"Engaged?" I must have blanched.

"He broke it off a couple of months ago and I just had to get out of Anchorage. Get away from him, from everything."

Women like to tell you they're engaged so you won't hit on them. It means they don't like you but they might like someone else. She came to me, sight unseen, on the rebound. She would feel sorry for me and Nightengale me so my miserable pain of living on wheels might go away. Why, she might even sleep with me just so's she could delivery a mercy fuck, and tell all her friends what she did for the poor guy she met through the advertisements in a magazine. God, this woman would be a challenge.

"Rachel," I said, "For whatever reason you came, I'm glad you did. "

She stood up, went to one of the bags she had brought in and withdrew an large manilla envelope. "Look," she said, "I've brought you a gift."

Rachel handed me a large drawing tablet, and I flipped through its pages. Wonderful renderings of wild animals danced on every sheet.

"These studies of sled dogs are terrific. "

She smiled. "I did them last winter when I worked with Mary Shields. She was wonderful. She let me play with her dogs and photograph them, and got me started on learning how to mush.

"Wasn't she the first woman to enter the Iditarod race between Anchorage and Nome?"

"She didn't win, but she showed the world what a woman can do. Mushings is not just a man's sport any more."

Rachel watched me for a reaction. "Maybe you'd like this one." It was a lithograph of a woman dressed in a white fur parka ascending a steep hill with her team. Snow, white as teeth, forming ruffs around gnashing boulders. Rider and team were silhouetted against the night sky scribbled with stars and lavender lights of the aurora borealis.

She saw me hesitate. "Here's one with a red-orange light in the sky. Take the one you like."

"That one." I pointed to a drawing of a musher and team going uphill. Sled marks and dog tracks were behind, but the driver had eyes only for what lies ahead.

"You picked one of my favorites. The Interior Light Gallery in Fairbanks handles my work. I've got a few things in Anchorage, Skagway and Juneau. I've had good luck with my wildlife studies. Actually, I'm having a hard time keeping up with the demand. I don't sell my dream series, but I'd be happy to give you one."

"It's not necessary." I didn't want to start out this relationship by being in her debt.

❑

She started unpacking immediately. I offered her another beer.

"Got anything diet?"

"What are you crazy, Lady? Sorry, no, but I'll get some next shopping trip," I said, wanting to please her. I retreated to my balcony ready to taste the best Bungadeen brewski in the world.

Rachel took a glass of water and went downstairs to her room to work.

At ten o'clock that evening, the sky was an electric blue, and McKinley reflected the pink clouds that nudged it. A barely perceptible lime-green glow separated the jagged Alaskas from the rest of the heavens. I closed my eyes and let the shadows chase the descending sun across the Tanana Valley in front of me.

Summers in Alaska wear a halo of light that make you want to get out and do and never quit. Last week the weather had been in the eighties, dropping to sixty or seventy in the bright evening light. Clouds like enormous pregnant mules strained across the sky. We were literally on the top of the world, a hour or so from the city of North Pole, with its giant sixty-foot-tall Santa Claus statue. Every year I was one of the volunteers that helped answer the thousands of children's letters that came in to Santa. Downstairs I heard the sounds of Rachel moving boxes around. The clouds delivered small likenesses of themselves. The hundred days of summer was well begun.

❑

"She's more than I bargained for," I said to my nearest neighbor and friend, Cary Penn, who lived a half-mile down the road. It was a few weeks later and I had invited him over for a taste test of my A-Number-One brewski, Bungadeen Blonde. Cary, a general practitioner and amateur body builder, looked like he could lift school buses. He had lived in Fairbanks for nearly ten years. His hair was dark and slick as automobile enamel, eyes that held everything, even light, within them. His hands were long and used to difficult work. Tongue in cheek, he claimed to be a "sourdough," a newcomer who had pissed in the Yukon, made love to an Eskimo and wrestled a grizzly bear. I figured he might have wrestled the grizzly. "Chechaquos" were new-comers who had yet to do these things.

"Your Rachel knows what she wants." Cary said with admiration. His face was that of a man becalmed on narrow waters. Grey hair the color of tin, eyes like the distillation of smoke.

"She's not my Rachel," I said, but I wished she was.

"She likes the house?"

"So far." I was proud of my house, bought it when I hit it big buying Microsoft stock, rode to the top and got out at the right time. I didn't know much about stocks, but my dad, who actively invested, gave me a hot tip, which by the way, he didn't take. So for a short while, I had made more money than he had saved up over forty years.

"She leaves here every day with a huge backpack and doesn't come back until almost midnight," I said.

"Anything going on between you?"

"It's only been a few weeks. I'm going slow. Anyway, why are you so interested?"

"Why not?" Cary said. "If you're not, I might be."

"Finders keepers in this game, my man."

"Maybe," he said. "Maybe not."

The house smelled vaguely of Rachel's perfume; a scent of roses and the oil paints she worked with down in her room. "She's not my Rachel," I said to myself.

❏

One day I rose early to go out "combat" fishing with Cary. I had a specially outfitted van and an electric ramp for the chair, so I could be pretty mobile. When the salmon and halibut run, folks are jammed into the streams, as tightly packed as a beehive and just as combative.

Rachel padded into the kitchen wearing a huge University of Alaska sweatshirt over a pair of shorts. "Mind if I borrow this? I found it in my closet." Her red hair popped up through the top of her visor hat. She threw down her backpack and started making herself a cup of coffee. Although she had a microwave and a refrigerator, she usually drifted into my kitchen to make an occasional meal.

"Sure, take it," I said. "Looks better on you then me. How about a beer? It's not just for breakfast anymore."

"Great idea," she said. "I'll take a bottle with me for later. I'm going off to meet Mary Shields."

"If you're going down to the Indian village on the Chena river, don't give them any of my beer," I laughed.

Rachel looked at me as though I was a severe nut case. "You've got a strange sense of humor," she said.

"How's the dogging?" I smiled. Women from New Yawk don't usually go out for mushing. They might freeze their fancy fingernails off. Oh, brother, don't think I didn't see her nail polish, intense as Alaskan poppies. And I noticed her lips, too. Always painted bright. And her eyes blazed like double kleig lights. A very attractive woman. It was easier to think it than to say it.

"Sledding, not dogging." she said.

I decided to be nice to her, just to keep her off balance. For Gods sake, she had her own tool kit! Pliers, hammer, wrenches, screw eyes, picture wire. She knew how to replace a broken floater ball in the toilet water tank and began fixing up stuff around the house. Suddenly, the hot water faucet in the bathroom worked better because she put a washer in it; hinges didn't scream for oil anymore; the toaster door didn't fall off every time I opened it.

Rachel yawned. She put her coffee down on a table and ran her hands through her hair. She had a very deliberate way of doing that, started on the top of her head and working down toward the sides, like she was giving herself a massage. "Got anything diet I could have?"

"Matter of fact, I do, and I handed her a Coke, secretly pleased with myself to have laid in a stock of them when Cary and I last went shopping together. Now there's something useful a man can do — go grocery shopping.

❑

One night, a few weeks later, I asked Rachel out for dinner and, surprisingly, she agreed. I hadn't put on a shirt and tie in a long time. I had to go through the usual precautions of calling to check out if the men's room was accessible; it's often easier just to stay home. It's not that I'm a loner, but I guess I had gotten in a rut. Between Internet classes and teaching at the university, I was pretty busy. Sometimes I went to the gym to lift weights and work some of the machines, sometimes had a couple of beers at the local bar. Mostly I met throw-away women in paper panties.

"You look nice," she said.

I saw myself as some kind of gigantic, incompletely formed lump.

"Handsome, even," she smiled at me.

We ate at a restaurant with an outdoor patio. The waitress had removed the dining chair from the table and I could slide my chair right in. I bless people who understand my situation and help without me having to ask for special attention. As Rachel spoke, the palomino sky raced on into dusk, the perfect moment of twilight, and we lingered late to watch the midnight sun.

"Have you been thinking anything about your future?" I asked.

"The future is only a step away," she said. When she allowed herself to take that step, she came back with nets full of futures, wriggling like ants on tarpaper, as though all she needed was the right net, the right trap, the right cage. And there would be a neon sign in the sky bobbing up and down in some unseen fluid that filled the heavens in search of people who could swim. Trying to understand it all was like trying to read a book in Braille wearing thick mittens. It was awkward but it could be done.

"Understand?" she asked.

I didn't really, but I liked thinking about what she said as she said it.

We drove back to the house and lingered over wine on the balcony for another fugitive hour. We watched the stars turn on and wondered whether there was life on other worlds.

"We can't be alone in the universe," she said. "Being here just confirms that belief. Everything is connected. I felt that the first time I saw the view from your home."

"Really? The view did that for you?" I was embarrassed that I hadn't gotten some deep emotional impact from the scene. After all, I'm part native, and I'm supposed to have this mystical attachment to the land, but I felt more at home working on my computer than going outside in the snow.

Rachel, outlined in the long glow of the evening, moved her chair closer to mine and said, "When I came to your house, I suddenly realized I had seen it before in my dreams. I began to have a certain dream when I was about ten, and it has continued all through my life with only slightly different variations. When I stood on your porch and saw the valley, the trees, and the mountains, I knew I had been dreaming about this place."

It must have been at least two in the morning, and the weather had taken on a chill. We made no move to leave.

She went on, "In my dreams I am looking at the stars. The sky is black with a red-orange mask, and I notice a strong light that I think is a star, but then it detaches itself and comes toward me. I'm not so much frightened as curious. The light gets brighter as it floats a vast whiteness, as white as milk. The sky gets darker, the lights in the sky get brighter. My heart is beating faster and I want to run, but can't. The light becomes stronger, and it turns out to be the headlight worn by the driver of a dog sled, a musher. He or she, I can't tell which, is wearing a head lantern that throws a light onto the dogs and the trail. Each little hair stands out like a silver wire. The musher stands on the sleds runners. The person is dressed in white fur and is intent on obtaining the rise of a snowy hill. I stand transfixed as the apparition passes by. I want to ascend with it, but I can't move.

"Waking from the dream was always the worst part. I wanted to follow the figure. I never told anyone, not even my folks, for years. Finally, I went to a psychologist because having the same dream over and over was beginning to get on my nerves. When I did that, the dreams became more intense, more detailed and progressive. Soon it became clear that the orange-red dancing lights in the sky must be the *aurora borealis,* and the place was Alaska. Mushing was about the furthest thing from my mind in New York, but the idea of aurora borealis changed all that. I decided I had to see the northern lights for myself. The second year I was here, I broke up with my fiancee, Alex and I saw your ad in *AlaskaMen.* So I answered it. You know the rest.

"I had another one of those dog sledding dreams last night. I am sleeping and I watch the scene: Everything is moving, like a landscape of white chickens. I can see the sled and the breath of the dogs, how their hair blows back, the big mittens of the driver, the scrunch of the snow underfoot. The driver is a woman, headlight glowing. She beckons me to jump into the sled basket. We take off. I feel like I'm airborne and the woman laughs and says *gee,* to make the dogs turn to the right. We begin to ascend a steep hill. There is something, someone waiting for us at the top of the rise. But then I wake up."

"Was the *aurora borealis* in the dream again?"

"Oh, yes. At first the sky was orange red, and then it slowly faded to other colors. In reading, I found out that red orange is unusual, but it does happen. About every eleven years. Its related to the sun-spot cycles. That's when they're at their height. The colors in the sky are caused by a solar wind of electrically charged particles.

"I think I've always known what I wanted to do. When I told my parents my decision about coming here to Alaska, they thought I was crazy, but they were supportive. Alex thought I was crazy, too, but he realized I had to do something with my life while he was away at sea. He's really a wonderful person, but we just can't seem to make our lives work."

"Breaking your engagement is tough," I said But it was great news for me. I felt excitement rising within me, some altogether irrational deep sense of gratitude that Alex hadn't the sense to hang onto Rachel. Thank God I had shaved that morning.

"I'm not the one who broke it," she said.

❑

"Rachel's going to live at my house through part of the winter," I told Cary on the way to see a movie at a theater that had been newly made wheelchair access. "She says she needs time to think."

"Well, its a great time to put some moves on Rachel," Cary said and I wondered who he meant, him or me. I was pleased she had decided to stay on a bit longer, and it wasn't just because her being a tenant would help pay the bills. She fell into the habit of joining me and Cary, and my twosome became a threesome. Carry invited himself in for long talks in front of the picture window that faced McKinley. He helped her patch a leak in the roof. He was crowding me.

The treetops that had been bent over a season ago were now standing straight and tall. Helen Shillart was teaching Rachel mushing, and Mary Shields helped her train a new batch of Malamutes. As for me, I started reading up on the *aurora borealis* by going to *Encarta,* an illustrated computer encyclopedia on

CD-ROM. It was a neat way to surf the information fields without freezing my ass off. I learned that the rapidly shifting streaks of light across the sky also occurred over Australia. It wasn't unusual for the phone line to have a lot of static on it when the colors were at their height. The auroral luminescence was caused by the solar wind whipping around high-energy atomic particles that originated in sunspots.

Rachel had threatened to dance naked in the backyard when she saw her first aurora borealis of the winter, but when it happened she settled instead for a hot jacuzzi. I was already steeping like hot tea when she came out on the porch in her robe. The air was cold and crackly, hovering around the zero mark.

"Don't expect me to be wearing a bathing suit or anything," I said, trying to be casual about it.

The breeze was silent as a fish as it pulled cloud tails across the sky. "Don't expect me to wear one either," she said and unconcernedly dropped her robe. The evening sun outlined her entire body in a brilliant light that curled over her face, dimpled her nipples and slid down to her toes. She entered the water quickly, leaving the nude image of herself in my mind.

Somehow warm water and cool stars make for nice conversation. "We never had a jacuzzi in New York," she said.

"Me, neither. We always lived in a small home here in Fairbanks. There's Norwegian and Athabaskan in me, but I never knew I was part Native American until I was in my twenties. My parents didn't want me to think of myself as a half-breed. So I guess you might say, I got cut off from that part of myself long ago. I'm not crazy about Alaska. I'd rather live in Florida."

"You're not giving this place a chance. You ought to come out sometime with me. I almost got my younger sister to come up with me this summer, but she's afraid of going places by herself."

"You've got to respect what other people are afraid of," I said. "I remember when I was growing up, I thought the bees I had killed would rise up to sting me, I would get sucked in by quicksand, break my head on the bottom of the pool, get my fingers caught in my bicycle spokes or a meat grinder, that I would get a rare and incurable disease from touching myself down there and I was always touching myself down there."

Rachel moved closer to me in the warm water. "I was afraid that dogs would bite me, that I would be struck by lightning, that mean boys would hang me by my braids from a tree branch. My mother said if I made a bad face it would freeze that way, and I have to admit, I was worried about that one, since I always made bad faces."

"It seems you have a more practical madness than mine," I said. "The worst scenario I could dream up when I was a kid — beyond garden variety monsters, bogey men, psycho-nuts, Freddy Krugers and horrific animals with split screen eyeballs — was the replacement brain/body horror. Either my parents would trade me in for a robot kid who looked just like me, wasn't me, but was nicer, or that I would get the brain of the dumbest kid in school and he would get mine."

Rachel clearly had never had such fears.

"Tomorrow, I'm going to go mushing under the stars, she said. I can just imagine the streams of the borealis jetting out like silver spikes seventy miles across the heavens. I'm going to wear a head lantern on the trail. I'll look just like the driver in my dreams with that get-up."

I could see the picture she had given me through the sliding glass door from my position in the jacuzzi. It was hanging on the living room wall. "Maybe I'll go with you."

"Are you kidding? You? I thought you said you weren't a nature boy. Just a man and his computer."

"Didn't your mama say not to believe everything a guy tells you?"

"If you come sledding with me, you could ride as a passenger. "

"I'll play the role of ballast," I tried not to feel sorry for myself.

"I think I can handle that," she said.

❑

I did go with her a week later, sat as a passenger on her sled. It was somewhere in the minus zero territory when we set out with Helen Shillart on the trail. The passenger seat was a little cramped for my long legs, useless as they were, and I wasn't used to speeding over the snow on a sled. Now and again we saw moose tracks, and mini-crevasses. I brought a hip flask of whiskey for warming, but Rachel said that alcohol makes you colder than it does warmer.

What started out as nebulous masses of indistinct lights in the sky slowly undulated into fans and flames, then curtains of luminescence. Sometimes Rachel and Helen shouted at each other, Helen giving Rachel instructions. Mostly it was quiet as the dogs pushed on. Occasionally she asked me if I liked it, as though she was a parent wanting to know if her child was having a good time.

I don't believe in things beyond knowing, astral bodies or gorilla hamburgers but as I was riding I remembered the drawings of Rachel's dreams, especially the one of the figure in the white parka driving the dogs against an orange sky. That was the print I had selected. She just called it number thirty-one in the dream series, but I thought of it as Ascending Angel because the figure had a certain ethereal quality, like a flare frozen inside an ice cube. Suddenly I knew how that figure had felt, how Rachel felt about what she was doing. It was as though the torch of an idea had been passed from her to me; as though I was a part of her landscape.

After the ride, I invited Helen to the house for hot toddies or hot chocolate, but she wanted to get on home. It was 2 AM, and the sun was climbing its ladder of light.

Rachel and I sat in the kitchen, talking. It was the perfect opportunity for me to take action. She was relaxed, happy, and sitting there before me, red cheeks, smiling. But somehow just because we had shared this house for over a half year, it was even more difficult to make a move toward her. She wasn't the kind of woman who smiles up at you, laughs and flirts. She didn't try to build up my ego; she didn't wear suggestive clothing. How could you wear revealing clothing when its minus fifteen? Rachel wasn't hesitant to talk about herself or to ask me questions about my life, and she seemed interested. But tonight's adventure gave me a new sense of excitement and I told her so.

She moved her chair closer, came over and planted a kiss on my lips, but backed off before I had a chance to return the favor.

"What did I do to deserve that?" I was pleasantly surprised. Maybe I was on the right course with her.

"You'll see," and she disappeared downstairs to her room. When she came back she was carrying a large cardboard carton. There, she said. "Open it."

She put the box on the table in front of me and I opened it. Inside were two husky pups. I picked them both up, and they began licking my hands. "Where did you get these?"

"Helen. She thinks I should raise my own dogs. Would it be all right with you?"

"You can't keep them here. I'm not a dog person," I said as the puppies nuzzled me.

"You will be," was all she said and put the puppies back in their box. "They are adorable, aren't they?"

"They are and so are you," I said grateful for the opening. She plopped herself in my lap and I pulled her toward me. I leaned forward and kissed her, and she did not pull away. She was wearing a big, bulky reindeer sweater and I put both hands under it and slid them up her back. Underneath the outer sweater, she wore a turtleneck. She responded to my embrace as though she had been waiting for it. I was puzzled but happy at the way she reacted. Then a thought hit me. "Say, is this a ploy to get me to keep those dogs here?"

"Such an idea never occurred to me," she said with a laugh. "But now that it has, how many kisses would it take?"

"You'd have to go for a lot more than kisses."

"Meaning?"

"Well, the roof needs fixing." I was kissing her nose.

"I could do that."

I ran my hands underneath the second sweater and she didn't seem to mind. "And I think the drain under the sink is clogged."

"Done. Anything else?" Her body was warm and inviting.

"I think my bed needs, uh, warming up."

"Why don't we go look at it?" she said and took hold of my chair and pushed it forward. "I hope it's nothing serious."

"It might be," I said when we were in my bedroom. "It might be worth at least one puppy, but I'm not sure."

Rachel sat herself down on the bed and slid out of her jeans. She was wearing bright blue jockey briefs. I wasn't surprised because that's the kind of underpants she wore under her big sweatshirts walking around the kitchen. Strangely, it didn't seem strange to be doing this with her. It was comfortable, and somehow different than bedding the women I had dated over the years. She was tall, with an elongated waist. There was nothing frail and demure about her. She took off her bra and slid into bed. I liked the way she looked at me from under the covers. I hoisted myself up onto the bed and began unbuttoning, unbuttoning everything, letting go of everything, but this is the part that always hurts for me; I see myself from my partners eyes. I watch me hauling myself up onto the bed like a sack of flour instead of a man. What can it be like to watch me, I wonder. Not inspiring. Where is Mr. Macho Man when I need him most? I have unbuttoned him and he has gone. I rolled in on top of her, and her whole being seemed to receive me.

"Everything is in working order," I said, wanting to reassure her as well as myself. This is the moment of truth, Bo Bungadeen. The more I worry about whether I can perform, the more likely

I won't. Maybe I was afraid Rachel wouldn't be able to accept me as I am.

She pulled my head down on her lips and we embraced for what seemed like a very long time. I suddenly felt a sense of warmth and acceptance from her that stilled the voices in my head. Suddenly, I wasn't worried about what to do next, everything began to flow. Then slowly as the evening sun sealed us together, we entered one another.

Later she asked, "Well, is that worth you letting the puppies live here or not?"

I was barely awake. "One, maybe."

"What would I have to do to earn the other one besides doing the sink and the roof?"

I hate it that women get so talkative after making love. "I'll think of something," I said and drifted off into a seamless sleep.

❑

Rachel stayed on all winter. Alex's tour was ending in a month and he had to decide whether or not he would stay in the Navy. Their relationship, as usual, continued to be an up-and-down thing and so I still had hope.

"If he decides to stay in the Navy, I have to decide if I can cope with that."

"Would you really give up your dreams for him?" I asked, wondering what kind of hold he had over her, that even in his absence through the long dark nights (to say nothing of my presence) that she could still be mooning over him.

"I've been in love with Alex for a thousand years. He's my first love—since highschool. He was on the football team, no not the captain, just a second stringer. We planned our lives together, everything was working out. I'm the one who suddenly changed the ground rules."

I guess she saw the look on my face as I listened to her.

"Bo, I don't want to hurt your feelings, I feel close to you. I think we could go on into eternity forever, but Alex always lives in the back of my mind."

I turned away from her and wheeled myself off into the kitchen.

Just before breakup, a time when the ice releases its grip on the land, and spring deliberates, I gave Rachel a book I had ordered on the aurora borealis for her birthday. It explained how electrons and protons penetrate the magnetosphere of the earth and enter the radiation belts, overloading it. She loved it.

Particles collide with gas molecules in the atmosphere and make them emit electromagnetic radiation in the part of the spectrum we can see. That's what makes the colors. "Isn't that wonderful?" She turned the pages rapidly to look at the pictures. That's what made her decide to go off on a solo mushing trek at night. She had her route marked off to Manly Springs and return. She wore her head lantern, and I thought she looked as though she was wearing a crown of candles as they do for Saint Lucias day at Christmas.

After we made love that first night, Rachel took up residence in my bed. The puppies, whom we named Brewski and Blondie, slept at the foot of the bed, and I was grateful for my new family. Rachel spent as much time as possible sledding and her enthusiasm and interest were rubbed off on me. She thought she could rig up some type of chair for me so I could take control of the sled. Every time I went with her I felt closer not only to her, but to my own roots.

"You're an angel, I said suddenly grateful to her as the dogs played at our feet. Just what's going to happen to us? What's the story with Alex?"

"You've been very patient. I'm trying to work things out. It'll all come to a head this week."

"Rachel, I don't want you to go."

"I know," she said and left it at that.

❑

Two days later, Rachel came into the dining room where I was trying to get a few bills paid.

"This is from Alex," she said, waving a letter before me. "He's decided to leave the Navy and he got a teaching job in engineering at the university here in Fairbanks. It's what I've been hoping for," she said sadly. "And now that its happened, I didn't even know he had applied to teach, I . . ." She didn't finish.

The bottom of my heart fell out. The early March day was a changeling child, not certain of what it would become or what was coming. Good weather made me feel worse. It would be a sorry business to live without her. My insides were in knots. The banished empty spaces returned to it.

"You're not really going to marry him, are you? We've been so great together."

"I'm sorry, Bo," was all she said.

❑

Rachel gave me several drawings as a good-bye gift. The sketches captured the wildness of each animal, the texture of the moon, the dithering clouds, the onyx tip of an ermine's tail. I turned to the dream series, and sifted through page after page of drawings of a figure in a white parka, color blanched from her face like something boiled too long. The driver nearly invisible against the white snow, moving uphill on the sled. The dogs eyes were fixed on the distant horizon. Who knows what the driver saw?

I looked at her drawings and remembered our time together. I remembered traveling on the sled and the unheard humming of animals and plants beneath the surface of the snow. Everything yearning for small release, some inner ease in the life, dark captives to seasonal migration, rising and setting of the sun. United not by blood or bones, but origins in star bangs and a universal song that each species carries for the sole purpose of being passed on so the next generation can learn to hum.

Now I sit on my balcony facing south toward McKinley, drinking Bungadeen Blonde, watching Brewski and Blondie play with each other in the dog run I built for them. The mountain squats on the horizon like an enormous white teepee. I wait for the darkness at midnight. A new dream has taken hold of me. It is like nothing I have ever dreamed before, but it has become repetitive.

A star is detached from a blood sky to become the head lamp of a musher, the driver and sled pass over the ice without effort, the snow is dirty and damaged, the color of old bones. I am dreaming of dogs and drivers become one, ascending a hill. Crisp is the snow, and the sky is like a speckled trout merging into one jammed whiteness, a stillness in the forest, tracks of animals who are not afraid, small lace patterns. An eternal whiteness none can own. A cold alchemical wind urges icebergs to new nesting sites.

I hear thunder-ice talk with a thunder voice, like someone bowling balls, like cannon fire, like electric cables snapping, a hum, a whine, an uncertain afternoon, small twigs humbling, gripping tree trunks as if to let go is to die. It is not cold in the coldness, just passing, all passing, all forgetting, all flying, a certain internal heat of what is seen and not seen in the ring world. I stand there, the dreamer who has never dreamt before; the land is dressed as a bride tossing snow-banks as memories, laughing under frozen waters. Brewski and Blondie run free beside me. I who have never dreamed must now warm to my task, must make a trail where there are no trails, must find the way when the path disappears, must send for the others when the danger is past, must share the load when the load is too much. I must not forget these things in the morning, when the sun shines and the dangerous night is done, and icicle prisons crack and drip life. Before me, so close come the dogs and driver all connected; their mummified breaths wrapped above them going up the hill, neither looking nor calling, all pulling. The driver's parka falls back and I see Rachel's face, an ascending angel and I am her passenger. And I know at last there are no limits to where the wings of desire may take her. Or me.

❑

80 Degrees North

The laws of nature seem suspended
Where glaciers chew the land
Into broken sculptures torn from unforgiving
    walls of ice.

Blue ice fingers grip the mountains,
    squeezing their cold throats.
Trees lock arms against the Viking winter.
Mountains wrestle the land down to its knees
Where houses stubbornly cling to earth
    like lint on dark jackets.

When summer comes, muttering clouds
Like old women having bad dreams
Stir from their long sleep.
The light stands at attention.
The sun leans out across the waters
And hesitates to kiss the ground.
Hides of islands,
Partially submerged leviathans,
    tread cantankerous waters.
The plaid sea's criss-crossed waves
Etch blue-veined maps that slice their milky way.
The fjords bristle with spiny hairs of shining ice,
And salmon laugh beneath the sea.

I started life in darkness,
Raised to sunlight,
A fragmentary life, a crystalline perception,
Uncoupled from the rest.
Set to drift upon the waters,
In a world that turns off center.
And in that silent occupation
Although far from home,
I am nearer to the incomprehensible.

❑

Song of the Cricket

THE DOOR SLAMS SHUT AND PHIL LOCKS IT FROM THE INSIDE. He springs toward me, right hand crushing my windpipe, left hand undoing his zipper, pulling my jeans down around my ankles, ripping my underpants.

"Down, get down," he whispers, pushing me backward toward the pile of rags on the floor.

His hand tears in between my legs; his finger shoots into me, then something else. He shoves himself into me. Hard. I hear a voice, Just lie there and take it. It's not the man's voice, it's my mother's. I remember that's what she said about sex, "All you have to do is lie there and take it. You won't die from it." She always said, "Whatever doesn't kill you makes you stronger." I hear her voice and it gets mixed up with mine. Well, she was right about one thing. I'm not going to die from this man on top of me with his crusty hair, his coffee breath and body odor like dirty socks.

My mind is elsewhere; disconnected from my body. I know I have to pass through ground zero, the center of the earth, before I can go back up again. When that happens, I'll be stronger. I'll have a plan.

❑

When I first came here, I would not tell the bearded doctor about how my husband David Wey left me and our daughter Leslie drowning in air. How David told everyone I was suicidal, how I tried to kill Leslie. They were lies to get me in here.

Dr. Menthol-Eucalyptus cleaned his glasses, stroked his Smith Brothers Cough Drop beard and sailed away on his black leather boat chair. His mouth opened and shut rapidly as though he was trying to catch flies, and the sound of his voice trailed after him, out of sync, like a bad actor in a poorly dubbed foreign movie. He looked beyond me, out the open window, past the grassy fields, past the trees that stood their ground like righteous prison guards.

"It was nice meeting you, Ann," he said on that first day.

Ann is my middle name; my real name is Amber, which I never use. Mom was reading her favorite novel, *Forever Amber*, when I was born. That's what she said when I asked her why she gave me that name. "It was that or 'Forever. So consider yourself lucky."

The doctor said, "I'll see you in a few days when you're feeling better."

"What, are you crazy, Doctor? Why would I ever feel better?"

❑

Dr. Methol-Eucalpytus said I should write everything down. Three weeks later he asked to see my journal and there was nothing in it.

"Why don't you write something, Ann?"

"Because you would want to see it," I thought, and kept still while everything whirled about me. White ceiling and walls and smooth, brown floors waxed and buffed every week. You won't die from germs in here.

I sat on my bed in the ward that night trying to make myself invisible. There is an annoying cricket somewhere in the room. I hate that cricket; and it hates me. It taunts me with its singing. If I find that cricket, I'll kill it.

The beds in the ward lined the wall, leaving a large open space which everyone avoided. What is there to fear in the center of a room? The beds were old, with white enameled head and foot boards. Black metal showed under the chipped white paint. Everything here was white washed, but something beneath the surface shone mean and cruel.

Dr. Menthol-Eucalyptus came right into our ward room for group therapy every other morning at ten. He called us patients, although the social workers were keen on the word "clients." Well, we were just nuts. I think he liked to call us patients because it made him feel more like a real doctor. But that meant, he didn't feel like a doctor. I think he felt more like a custodian watching over unhatched eggs. Birdlings, who must break their shells if they are to come out into the world. The doctor, who smelled like menthol-eucalyptus cough drops, tried to get me to speak, but I sat quietly with my hands in my lap and let the other patients make fools of themselves. They spoke and I listened, thinking to myself how once the shell is broken, there is no choice but to come out.

Dr. Menthol-Eucalyptus would make a circle of chairs in the dead-space in the center of the room, and I would sit picking my toes. It was about the only thing that got to him. If I did it long enough, he would say "Don't," in a voice that admitted he had broken one of his own rules. That's my game, break the rules.

❑

I had a doll, Raggedy Ann, since I was a child and still had her when I married David. I thought Id give it to my own little girl, someday. That little girl turned out to be Leslie. David said I should throw Raggedy Ann out. I pretended to give the doll to Leslie, but she was still mine.

Leslie! I hope your grandma remembered to make your lunch for day care.

❑

A few months ago, I started writing about the doctor trying to hatch eggs. But I wouldn't show it to anyone, except for Mandy, a woman in my ward with a stringy smile, who yesterday said, "That stuff you write is shit." Yet she gave me a kind smile (OK, a smile that lacked a few teeth, but kind nevertheless) and we sat together at lunch.

Our lunch was always mashed up something; mashed potatoes and mashed soup. The staff was stupid, Nurse Polanski above all. Well meaning, but poor doing; every day she wore a different flower handkerchief stuffed into her breast pocket along with her breast. She watched me from the corner of her eye as though I was some kind of wart that must be burned away.

Wouldn't you be surprised, Nurse, if you knew I saw you staring at Dr. Menthol-Eucalyptus? How you blush when he's around. Polanski once told me that the doctor got his degree from a diploma mill, so he could keep his pay scale, not his education, up.

Life keeps getting more serene,

When you fly on thorazine.

❑

The sunlight shatters on the waxed floor of the day room where I keep track of time by spilling water on the floor. It takes an attendant two minutes to clean it each time. Six water glasses to an hour, six hours to a day, six clouds to a year. I am pouring time from one container into another. How long am I here? Let's see, it was last September that I came and now it's April and the cricket has been sucked into the Bermuda Triangle.

After I was here awhile, Dr. Menthol-Eucalyptus said I could go to art therapy.

❑

This is a factory where they manufacture crazy people, but therapy will fix me up. What is therapy? Group therapy (sit in circles and talk in circles), poetry therapy (what rhymes with shit?), work therapy (scrub the floors), horticulture therapy (weed out dead plants on the hospital grounds), bibliotherapy (read a book, Baby, and keep your fucking mouth shut), and art therapy (color your grief green).

There are two art therapy rooms here at Overbrook, the New Jersey State Mental Hospital. Overbrook is over no brook. I suggested changing the name to Over-no-brook, and Polanski almost laughed.

This is a red brick fortress with long corridors, crumbling paint and underground tunnels. Miles of corridors in the half light. The inmates float along the walls seeking their way through a maze, feeling their way though the labyrinth. They swim through the corridors, pale denizens of the deep, bottom feeders, rendered harmless, strung out to dry. This would be a good place for torches and a torture chamber.

The people are mostly older than me, white-haired, scruffy, waiting for their time pill. Waiting to be zonked so they won't feel anything. It was the young ones in their twenties like me who were scary to look at. I saw myself echoed in their faces. We were not wrinkled or lined or hunched. We could play basketball, go skating or bike riding. We could, but we don't.

❑

It was getting on toward summer.

"Do you feel better, do you feel better?" my mother would ask whenever she came to visit, mincing along in high heels that made stiletto holes in the grass. The bare sides of her feet always had green stains. Her electric orange hair was pulled back at the nape of her neck. Arcs of energy emanated from her head, spiraling across her dangling earrings, the kind you're not supposed to wear past a certain age.

She's getting older and its hard for her to take care of Leslie. She always brings me a box of candy when she comes. I don't like candy and she knows it.

"Really, you don't want it? Such nice candy, a *Whitman Sampler.* My favorite kind. I would've thought you'd love the nougat centers."

"No, you keep it, Ma," I would say and she would look at me with these little cats eyes narrowing to a point. Eyes that made you feel she was going to spring at you any minute.

"You look great, you'll be out of here in no time. You know they can't keep you in if you want to get out, that's the law."

"No, I didn't know that's the law." Maybe she's just saying that to get me to come home and take care of Leslie. Some days I think I'd like to do that. David hadn't been around since last September when he had me dumped here. Left Mom to look after Leslie and pay his bar bills.

The last time she was here, Mom put the lid on the candy box, slipped a huge rubberband around it, put it back in a torn A&P shopping bag, and rose up high on her summer sandals. Her toes were painted Fuchia Rose. She gave me her leftover bottle of polish.

"And when you come home, don't try to kill yourself," she said searching her purse for bus change. "It's not worth it."

I think she was trying to say she did not want to have to clean up a mess in the bathroom and wash out the rug if that's where I tried it.

Staring out the lobby window, I watched her take a shortcut across the grass to the bus on Route 5. Crickets and grasshoppers jumped at her with displeasure as she dislodged them from their secret haunts. She let her jacket fly open in the warm spring air, holding the box of chocolates to her chest. Surely they would melt by the time she got home. Those crickets, they sing day and night, whether they have a reason to or not.

❏

There is something in the wind that comes unbidden. A temporary clearness where your mind sees straight, and the voice that you hear is only yours, humming against itself, dividing up the clouds. It is your voice and your voice only, though it may come cloaked as your mother's or your father's—or even a cricket. It is your voice, crying alone and looking for comfort in the steel cage of your thoughts and the pinprick of consciousness. When you hear it, you know you're better.

My voice is a Hansel and Gretel trail that leads out of the dark woods to a place of refuge, a gingerbread house that turns out to be the office of Dr. Menthol-Eucalyptus.

❑

The art therapy rooms were beneath the main building, directly below the admitting office. To get there you went down with a nurse in a locked elevator. We were moles trapped under the earth. The peeling painted elevator door slammed shut, and we shot down to the interior, followed endless corridors, passed shuffling groups of people led by white-jacketed attendants.

Take a right, a left, two rights. A wrong turn and you ended up in the storage room, the laundry room, or the garbage area. They treat you like something that needs to be hidden.

"We will all end up in the garbage can or under a white sheet," Mandy said when I told her how trapped I felt.

"No one's going to take me out of here that way," I said and bit down softly on my tongue. "The only way I'd let them do that is I'd pretend to be dead, and they would wheel me right out of here, and I'd have a car waiting on the other side, and I'd jump into it. Ha ha. That'd be good. I saw that in a movie once, and it worked fine."

"Sounds like a great plan," she said, pleased because she had seen the same movie. "Could I go with you?"

"Sure. My ideas are always big enough for two."

❑

Spanish Eyes, one of the two art teachers, waited for us. She laughed, showed mismatched teeth. She waited under the bowels of the building in a windowless room lined with plumbing pipes that hung like raw sinews from the ceiling. Spanish Eyes, the art therapy lady, hardly spoke English; that's why they got her cheap. Birdlike, she would cock her head and chirp at us. She always wore jeans with tight sweaters and enormous gold earrings. Her dark eyelashes were like bars in mascara prisons. How I wish I had Spanish Eyes for my teacher, but instead I was assigned to Phil.

The tip of his nose quivered when he spoke. His hands were the size of oven mitts. He wore the same old green sweater all the time. It was loosely woven, frayed and pilled. I kept thinking if I could pull one end of the yarn, it would all unravel and there would just be a puddle of green yarn on the floor.

"You sit there," he said to each of us that first day in his studio and he assigned places at the table as though we were chess pieces, inanimate objects on his game board.

Suddenly, I heard that cricket again. It must have followed me, must have risen from the Bermuda Triangle just for spite. It chirped incessantly as the ten of us sat in his art room at a long table covered with cracked oilcloth the color of chalk dust. We had crayons, some watercolor boxes and charcoal. Marie was there, a woman who knitted her husband a sweater and when he put it on for the first time, stuck him in the heart, through the sweater, with an icepick. Marie never painted, she just sat there clicking her needles, knitting. Mandy usually sat next to me; she was a "chronic." Jessie, who spoke with a strange baby lisp, sounded like she was spitting when she said something. She liked to draw cats' eyes.

None of them minded that I didn't speak for a long time but they didn't mock me or give me special attention, which was too bad.

"Ann doesn't talk much," Jessie said to the others sitting around the art table. That's all the special treatment I got.

"Here's the paper," Phil said. His eyes leapfrogged over my body. His eyes were slits, heavy-lidded slits so deep in his face he could see backward and forward at the same time. Ears with lobes so large they looked like earrings.

He touched me on the shoulder. I felt the imprint of his palm long after he removed it.

"What is art therapy?" I asked.

"You draw a picture," Phil said, keeping his voice steady, meaning it was not his job to explain. His tone meant I would get it when I should get it, like when you meet the right man you are supposed to know it. I thought David was the right man and married him, but he pushed me around, stole my last dollar, beat Leslie, left her at Mom's and was out of my life.

"Is it crazy to want to kill yourself if you have no money and no future?" I asked Mom.

"There's always a future," Mom said, "just not always the one you'd want."

❑

The doctor asked a lot of questions about my ex, as though it mattered who he was, who I was, and why did I take his crap all those years? I fell in love with David because he was good-looking, did bird calls, and played piano in a bar. The day before we got married it seemed like enough; the day after it wasn't. Then we had Leslie. I used a diaphragm, but she snuck by. The doctor said that maybe I didn't put it in right.

Maybe.

I'm writing all this down for evidence.

❑

"Draw a picture, Ann," Phil commanded.

I did not know what to draw.

"Do cats' eyes," Jessie advised and flipped her bangs off her forehead. She drew twenty cats on her paper, all with enormous fringed eyelashes and twirling, impatient tails. I heard Jessie had a crush on Spanish Eyes and got kicked out of her art room. She had been drawing cats' eyes ever since.

Mandy said, "You're right to be careful about what you paint." She looked from my blank paper to Phil and back to me. "They know everything about you by what you draw. Don't throw anything out. I saw Phil pick stuff out of the wastebasket to look at it. Don't draw people; they can tell a lot by that."

If I didn't talk to people, I wouldn't draw people. So I drew a picture of my doll, Raggedy Ann, who was at home with Leslie. The doll had black button eyes that saw everything, a painted mouth, and wore red and white striped stockings. She had on a white pinafore, and under her blouse used to be a heart that said, "I love you." The night before I came to Not-so-Overbrook, I cut out her heart with a razor, so Raggedy Ann will love no one but me. Then I cut myself with the razor in a few places to see if my blood was as red as her stockings, and David found me bleeding in the bathroom. Leslie was asleep. He put me in this loony bin and after that David was gone.

Every time Phil came by he ran his fingers, along the top of my shoulders, with just enough pressure to make the little hairs on the back of my neck quiver. His touch carried a meaning.

❏

The days went by sometimes in clumps, sometimes not at all. I drew row on row of fortresses, moats, towers and bridges. I was chained in the highest tower behind a locked door, waiting for my prince. I drew long blonde hair for myself (my real hair is short and curly and black). I was afraid to close my eyes because if I did, I would lose my balance and fall into the hole in the center of the earth and go to China. But the question was, how do you go up from China? Phil read my thoughts as I read his. Mine were pasted on my forehead.

❏

Nurse Polanski came with the dawn and the dark with her pill cart slushing on the cold wax floor dealing out forgetfulness like trump cards. In my dreams, her smiles were upside-down screams, and I fell into the water, fighting upstream. I saw the patients floating in the underground grottos in a startling blue phosphorescent haze. I swam past a group of women in sea-weed dresses making an intricate patchwork quilt underwater. They didn't notice me though I was screaming. Dr. Menthol-

Eucalyptus treaded water in his black chair boat. I was doing a lot of yelling and my throat hurt.

I told the doctor about my dream. "You are swimming for your life," he replied. He said he was encouraged about my progress and wrote notes on my chart. He was not the one screaming or drowning.

I feel a little better. This must be therapy. Then one day, while I was on the shore screaming, he asked, "How are we today?" Who did he mean by *we?* Was he including himself in *we?* How could I know how he was and why didn't he? I continued screaming.

"Keep it down," the doctor said, hinting of dark pastures and heavy sleep.

❏

I fantasized that I slipped out of my chains and jumped off the tower of my castle the other night because unless I do, they will keep me here forever. This hospital drains the blood of people. Whenever a new patient came, they took an old one, broke her and threw her bones in the storage room. They called this getting well. It's lucky there were always people in line waiting to come in. Lucky for the nurses, attendants and doctors, the cooks and the clerks. Without us, they would have no jobs, so they have plenty of reasons to keep us crazy.

❏

I cried the whole day through.

"You're improving," the doctor said. His real name was Dr. Bernard. I always knew that.

"Polanski told me you went to a university in a closet," I said. "That the only thing real about your education is the ribbon on your diploma."

Bernard laughed his head off. "That woman never did like me," he said. But under his laughter I thought I caught a glimpse of anger toward her, and maybe a little more respect for me.

"Read me something from your journal," he said and I read a poem about the cricket. I wrote it even though I did not attend poetry therapy. You are allowed to write poetry, anytime, just like you are allowed to live it.

Song of the Cricket
by Amber Ann Wey

To suffer is to feel the bite of the cricket
Long after the cricket is dead
And his song has been sung.

One can find other crickets that bite
And their songs will live in ones brain forever.
That crickets cannot bite is beside the point.

The doctor listened. "I disagree with part of what you wrote," he said. "That crickets cannot bite seems to me to be exactly the point. If you think you were bitten by something that doesn't exist, you're living in a fantasy world."

"And that," I said, "is my point. And I'm not changing it."

❑

I went to art class regularly after that, although I still didn't like Phil. He had no training, no education and no qualifications for art therapy other than that he was once a patient himself, worked cheap, ate little. During that time he had done remarkable drawings, showing in exquisite detail how he had been abused by his parents. He had been in the hospital for almost twenty years and when he emerged from his dark cocoon, he found his family and friends gone. He had no one to abuse him anymore and he missed it. He stayed on at the hospital as an "assistant" in the art room for a very small salary. I got this from Mandy, who it turned out, had been a patient along with Phil. She told me everything about this place.

Phil was tall, perhaps six foot two or three and nearly fifty years old. He knew the movements of everyone by sound; he did not have to be looking at us to tell when or where we moved. His mouth had a slight quiver. Thin, graying hair, flecks of yellow straying across colorless eyes that contained a certain kind of power waiting to be released. He always stood very close to us and leaned over us as he studied our work. He liked to rub up against us. I was not imagining it. He smelled from lint, aftershave lotion, and curious desires.

It was near the end of my last summer at Over-No-Brook that it happened. Mom was mad when she left that day. I asked her to leave the box of chocolates and I ate all the nougat centers.

Then an attendant took me down to the art class. I remember it quite well. No light filtered into the art room because there were no windows, and the sulky heat made the room more stifling and hotter than usual. Jessie was pouring herself a cup of coffee. That was one nice thing about Phil. He supplied coffee and donuts all day long. A new cricket hiding in the overhead pipes had come to haunt us. Mandy sat in her chair and rocked, and there were several old-timers around. I had gotten used to speaking with the others, even the staff on occasion. I was writing down my thoughts. I made pictures of the inmates; pale worm-like things beneath the earth; bleached and beached.

I needed some more drawing paper and Phil put his hand on my shoulder, oh so lightly. Told me to go into the storeroom outside our art room to get it.

❑

Now I'm back at the beginning, in the storeroom. I screamed and hollered and acted like I was going out of my mind as soon as Phil opened the door and grabbed me. As a parting shoot, I kneed him in the groin and he doubled over. I started screaming and yelling and making a hell of a fuss. So did he! An attendant came running and Phil bawled out that I attacked him. The guard packed me off to the doctors office. I was heaving, angry, and mad.

"Dr. Bernard, Phil told me to go to the storeroom for the paper. I went to the back of the room for supplies. Phil came after me. He slammed the door shut, and locked it from the inside. Why does he have a lock on the inside of the store-room?" I am in a cold sweat.

Bernard sat there, eyes floating over his appointment calendar. "Sit down," he said.

I stood in front of him; I would not sit. "'Get down,' was all Phil said, 'Get down.' Over and over he said it, and pushed me onto the pile of rags. 'Get down,' he said, 'I can kill you easy.'

"I felt sick to my stomach. 'I'll scream, I'll report you. They'll send you away for a long time,'" I yelled.

"But he only said 'Shut up.' He pressed my windpipe hard enough to convince me he would gladly break my neck. I started crying in pain.

"His mouth covered mine, his hands bit into my breasts with ragged nails. He pinched my nipples hard. He covered my mouth and stopped me from calling for help.

"'You love it, you want it. I'm giving you what you want.'" He pulled off his pants. His breathing came faster." I paused. I felt my tears sizzling on my red hot cheeks. "Should I say all the details, Doctor?"

Dr. Bernard finally looked up from the scattered papers on his desk. His eyes shone with a kind of a glaze as though he was seeing everything I described. Black boat chair creaked. "How do I know you didn't seduce poor Phil? He's an easy target."

I suddenly became enraged, startled to hear my voice so strong and clear. I stood in front of the doctor, leaned over the desk and grabbed him by the tie.

"You sick son-of-a-bitch, you think I'm making this up? You think I wanted that creep to touch me?" I yelled. A white-hot wire of anger arcs through my body, everything flames up.

"I gave Phil a present in the groin with my knee that he'll long remember. I'm going to close down this place, that fucking art room. You'll never subject me or anyone else to therapy again! I'm leaving, I'm leaving, I can go anytime I want to."

I ran down the corridor, tears streaming down my face, heart beating so wildly I think it will pop out of my chest. I can smell Phil all over me; it is all I could do not to gag. And suddenly I have a future and a plan. Even if I have no money, I have hope, and I will not be carried out in a white sheet. Even if it kills me, I am running away, not so much from this place of confinement but toward myself, toward my new voice and a healing that had begun, but would never be complete.

❏

Cricket

Medium Rare

I shut the door on my kitchen where
Serious swatches of wallpaper hang askew.
I hoped to get an artistic consensus,
    but nobody agrees about anything,
Least of all me.
I am floating in my pool, in that dead space
    between the kitchen and
The dog house, where the spiny cactus dildo grows.
I have slobbered the suntan oil on my
    white whale body.
My blowhole vacuums in the water
    and farts it out again.

I am entranced by the pool sweep —
    carrying around its own bag of dirt.
The carved wood clouds are eating up my day, one by
    one making all my time obsolete,
    chewing on my lethargy.
I press my sautéed body in the floating mat.
I am plastic wrap, floating on the surface of the water,
    seen but unseen, surrounded by
A fireweb of waves that suck my toes,
    ripples of my own good charity.

There is cancer in the sun, in the sky, in the water,
  and the *Sparkletts* man cannot fix it.
I am in my dog house in the water,
    memorizing the sunlight as though it will be turned
    off at four. For good.
I see the strawberries growing where the dog peed, but
That little patch of brambles
    which I so carefully nurtured are all
Dead now.
The chaparral squeaks up the hill,
    leached grasses lusting after water.
They cannot drink from my pool.
The chlorine would kill them.

Do you think if I had a prick I could write with it
    like a man,
Or would I be just another interior decorator
    worrying about wallpaper?
No sir, I write with my tits and scratch my ass,
And try to disregard the queen of Toshiba
    who laughs in my face.
Fruited wombs of sunlight cut sharp shadows
    on the red tiled roof,
And the sky sizzles while clouds piss away their rain.
Every body's gotta go sometime or other.

Children cry beyond the gate.
Civilization will come down with a big net
   and pop them in the
Animal Protective Van and take them away,
   like they promised with the raccoons.
The animal man in the animal van had a long pole
   for lassoing the raccoon.
He struggled like a hive of angry bees, but in the end
The animal man dropped him through the trap door
   of the van.
He sez he will take the raccoon to the furthest
   end of the valley where the
Malibu-boos live.
But I think he just release the raccoon at the bottom
   of my driveway
So he can trudge up my hill again.

I wonder if there is a trap door at the bottom of my pool,
   where I can go without drying off first.
Would my degrees float to the bottom,
   or are they stitched on my head?
What lies beyond the garden and the whir
   of a lawnmower edging my soul?

I am looking at the sky over my house,
It punctures all the corners where I hide.
The phone cord creeps after me like a Slinky.
If I could live in the water, I would train the fish
    to take messages.
The pavement is a sightless square,
    embedded crystals false prophets of cement.

Such a little prison with its comfort coves.
I will float till midnight here so I can see the tails of stars
And merge into their solitary waves, those lines
    of connection that tie me to them.
The gate is open now, the children sleep,
    the gypsy caller sings to me.
Tonight I will float face down.

❑

Killer Shoes

I found the killer shoes hiding on the sale rack.
They were my size. Sculptured open-toed,
Backless patent leather platform pumps
With a cunning heel wrapped in silver and black.
The clear plastic vamp
Exposed a quick flash of my naked foot
As it slipped into its transparent cage.

The shoes were not what I was looking for.
They were looking for me.
Shark shoes that could cut through water
With only their fin tips showing,
Ready to slash through Hush-Puppies,
Reeboks, and Oxfords,
Dismembering and devouring them.
Cosmic shoes, sucking up energy like a black hole,
A thirsty alchemy filled with rage.

Shoes like this could swallow the universe whole.
I put on my kismet shoes and catch my reflection
In every silvered mirror.
When I grow too old to totter on their four inch heels,

I will have them bronzed,
Embedded in a Lucite cube
Or cryogenicaly frozen,
Even the scent of them
So that I might
Savor my killer shoes again
In the next millenium.

❑

In the Interest of Science

WHEN WE GIRLS WERE BOTH NINE I asked Cricri (it sounds like Cree Cree) about what she was doing with the boys out in the woods in back of my house. Cricri was my friend Christine's nickname.

All the homes in our neighborhood in Boonton, New Jersey, had big backyards with no fences, and you could walk through the woods to each other's houses. You couldn't see the back of anyone's house when you started out, you just had to believe that (like most things in life) they were there. The neighbors' homes always appeared just when you thought you were lost, when you thought you might have been headed, by mistake, toward the lake and the gun club. You thought you might be mistaken for a deer if you wandered off course, and hoped you wouldn't die from an early bullet.

The houses on the other side of the woods, did spring up, like New York does when you come up at it from the Jersey side and go round that bend in the highway, and you think, "nah, it doesn't exist," and then suddenly you saw the city inflated in the distance and the gummy clouds that loped over the tops of the tall buildings and the water and sky met as if they couldn't decide which one would be which.

Then vroom, you'd get sucked into the Holland tunnel. White tile walls sweated smooth and damp. Then you'd see this guard sitting in a booth so small it looked pasted on him. I remember that once on the Garden State at Christmas time, some toll booth keeper threw a bunch of lollipops into the car. Not one, but a dozen or more, every flavor; cherry pops and orange, and even root beer. It never happened again.

When you crashed out of the tunnel and turned uptown, there were the black plastic garbage bags hanging out on the curbs, and the people clicked by, and if you took a wrong turn you might get the bullet you missed in New Jersey. I think they made a movie about getting lost in New York with Jack Lemmon.

❑

Cricri told me that summer when I asked what she was doing with the boys, that she took Duane to the edge of the woods that lapped at my house's backyard, just inside the thickness where trees grew in hot profusion and summer spilled all over everything. Winter or summer you couldn't see into the forest that grew between the houses.

My parents were adding a new wing and bathroom onto the house. The construction seemed to go on for years, and it felt that the house was being gnawed on. Cricri and I liked to play with my dollhouse downstairs in the rumpus room. And that is what I liked best: having fun with Cricri.

Cricri said she did it with Duane when he was six and she was nine. She had him pull down his shorts and looked at the little button that grew down there, and she told him he was growing a mushroom! And she put it in her mouth and licked it.

It didn't have any taste, she said, or any smell, it was just this funny round button. She licked it, and she liked it, and it got a little bigger in her mouth, though not by much, not so's you could hardly notice. And Duane brought his friend Tommy along next time, and they both liked what she did there in the deep green of the woods.

"I would like to do it too," I said. Not really. I had seen boys' things before. I saw one on my cousin Barry when he was a few months old, and I thought of touching it with my mouth, just because it was cute.

You wouldn't tell your mother this, would you? Of course not, and neither did I. I brought this up to Cricri the other day when our kids had gone off to nursery school. She was kneading bread and I was watching her while I sipped a cup of coffee made with steamed milk from the expresso machine. We're still friends after all these years the way friends are when their childhoods merge. We liked to discuss the old days because it kept burnt memories alive, because each of us could contradict the other's lack of faith that certain things really happened.

Cricri remembered quite well. She never forgot anything important, like how good the grass smelled in its damp jacket in the woods, the look of green sunlight, and newspapers and fire pits and fried ants and mud pies and white chunks of gravel. We saw the tree's fiery breath trying to scorch the birds that shot across the twilight sky. We lay down on top of dirt and leaves to watch the clouds and the sunset, and put our heads on rocks that became soft as pillows. Cricri said soft rocks was a crazy idea, that's why she liked it.

I've sucked on a man, as a grown woman, of course, but I never did it with a man in the woods. And I never told anybody that once Cricri made me nibble on Tommy in the Crime Car. We were laughing and walking toward the lake that afternoon, even though it was hunting season and the "No Trespassing" signs were new again. I was scared, and afraid of stumbling on dead deer more than getting shot myself.

The Crime Car was the 1936 Black Ford hidden deep in the woods in back of my house. You couldn't see it resting there even in the midst of winter when all the trees were bare, because their silvery branches were so close together. We liked to go look at the car in the winter, too. Our footprints were the only vistors the car ever had, and it seemed to us, though of course this was silly, that the car moaned when we left it.

Most of the kids who lived in the neighborhood knew about the Crime Car, but we never told our parents because the automobile was so creepy. There it stood, tall trees all around it, evanescent sunlight filtering down on the dull black enamel. The windows were cracked or blown out. I thought I could see a bullet hole on the driver's side. Everything was intact but decaying. The gray upholstery was full of leaves and squirrel droppings. The driver's door had fallen on the ground, the other doors were wide open, inviting us in. But I had never gone inside until this particular afternoon. It felt like the ghosts of the bad guys were still there, watching what we were doing. In the summer, we liked to walk through the woods to the car, making sure we didn't touch the poison ivy that grew in profusion all around us. Then we'd take out our sandwiches and cans of Coke, and just sit in front of the car like we were worshiping it.

So, on this late afternoon, Cricri took Duane, me and Tommy to the Crime Car and we drank our Cokes and we shuddered to think about how and why that car got there. It looked even bigger when you sat in front of it, and we thought we could almost see our warped reflections in the metal. When Cricri finished she went over to Tommy and whispered and he had a funny look on his face, like "OK, but I dunno," and they both got up and they actually went inside the car and I couldn't believe that she did that, and she said, "Come on, it's OK," and she pulled down his pants and he sat on the back seat and she knelt in front of him and right there in front of me and Duane she started playing with, uh, Tommys thing. She smiled at me like she was sharing her best jewelry, and she looked at me with her soft eyes and the boy got hard and then she let him go and his thing stuck, out straight, pointing the way to the lake. And so right then, she made me do it, it was her idea that I should put him into my mouth, and in kind of a way, I wanted to, but I didn't want to. But I did. So I stepped into the car to show I was like Cricri. Not afraid of him, or the car, or the bad guys. And it was like a science experiment because nothing bad happened, and I knew I could do it again.

His thing was still warm from her mouth, and popped out like an accordian, and it felt, well, slippery, like an uncooked hot dog, and smooth. I kept my eyes shut so's I wouldn't have to see anything, but every now and then I looked at Tommys face to see his expression.

He was just having a good time, smiling and everything. Why did we do those things? We told ourselves we were just trying out our bodies to see how they worked and whether we liked working them. And it being in the interest of science, why I thought it was all right, too, but kind of overrated as an activity, because I did not care all that much for hot dogs.

When I got through with Tommy, he got out of the car, and pulled his pants down, and peed out in a high arc; the droplets caught the top rays of the sun and sparkled and fell to the ground like amber diamonds, and he zipped up, and the sun came down, and we all ran back to my house and you could still hear the hammering and the wheels of construction trucks going up and down my driveway. And a toilet was sitting out on our front lawn.

Until today, Cricri and I never talked about that afternoon, but I have done that very thing to some guys, not a lot. Just some special ones, though I never cared much for it. I can do it if I think of those little boys, it kind of charges me, and I can do it now with my husband if I've had a good day with him, and he's nice to me, but after you're married you're kind of limited on how many days there are like that.

❑

Now Cricri is making a three strand braid of bread and is talking about oral sex. All she says on the subject is it's power over men and go for it, what in hell is wrong with you? Give the poor bastard a blow job and he's putty in your hands.

For me it's submission. I finally figured it out, it's doing the thing he wants you to do, and I've had enough of that. Especially if we had an argument and we usually do. No, I don't think I start the quarrel. Maybe I do to avoid the blow job, but it's the kind of thing I can't force and Cricri says, "You're a genuine nut case. You're sincere enough to fake liking it, so pretend you're not submitting. Think about the meaning of that thing in your mouth."

I said, "What meaning? Submission is what I think," and she said maybe there's something more to it.

"More? How could there be more to it?"

"It's his Achille's heel. Think if you had to kiss a man's foot. It's much better located where it is."

"I don't like to drink it," I said. "Tastes like egg whites. Makes me gag."

"Well, that's close. It's sperm whites. It's seed. Are you afraid they'll grow in your stomach?

"No, just afraid I'll throw up."

"I don't find it half bad," said Cricri, and laughed.

Now that we're grown up, we think we can call things what they are, as though by having the right word we have captured the thing itself. But the word was never quite right because you can never say exactly what you meant.

Cricri continued, "I like it when he puts his finger into me and touches that spot way inside. If he does it enough, I feel so great. Uhmm. I imagine I'm in a garden, outside of myself but inside of myself and if he says something in a certain tone of voice, then the gates to a garden open and I find myself involved, and time doesn't exist, and the two of us are wrapped in each other, downside up and upside down, and something breaks in me, something moves in me, and I want more. As for putting him in my mouth, it's almost like a pacifier, something to hold on to."

I've had that feeling, I admit, very rarely lately with my husband, Douglas, although it happened quite a bit in the early days before I found out that he was everything I expected him to be. And even then I didn't like to swallow. And he insisted on looking into me from the bottom up, and I felt as though I was on an examining table in a doctor's office. Appraised. Nothing secret anymore. I don't want him to know everything about me, see everything."

"You are the container," Cricri said, "as well as the contained." She always said things like that, but in this case I understood that I could hold all that Doug was, to draw him like a dark vessel to contain him.

Cricri stopped talking, put a wash of egg white on the bread and sprinkled poppy seeds on top. She brushed flour off her white skirt. She wore sheer dresses in the summer time, the kind your mom always told you to wear slips under, but she doesn't.

I would like to wear a gauze dress and take Douglas into the woods. "Pull down your pants," I would say, or perhaps I would say nothing and just make love to him. Perhaps I'd go straight for that soft pouch, just to harden it up, maybe I'd mouth it a few minutes. Then I'd run off with him toward the lake, and I'd remember the house of my childhood not far from where we live now. I'd remember that time in the Crime Car with Cricri, Duane, Tommy and the pounding on the house, and the toilet sitting on the front lawn for the longest time.

I'd remember that day long ago, when the forbidden was bidden: how the boy looked, his penis dangling and slender and more than a little surprised, but I never think of that now, only on warm days when there is no breeze. It's on that kind of a summer evening I imagine I hear the sound of hammering and pounding and the woods invite me and the green of the leaves go clapping, the red-tipped sun is setting and the rocks are soft.

❑

Changing History

I AM WAITING FOR LAURIE TO COME. We were friends in high school and I've got to admit she's a lot better looking today. For most people I think, the effect of time moves the opposite way, you're good-looking when you're young, everything stands up—or out—straight, but with time, everything slumps. Not so for Laurie, who stands taller, laughs heartier. Shes not afraid to laugh now because she had the space between her teeth bonded.

I move the shopping bags under my feet, and try to smooth out my red shirt. It has popped out of my skirt again. I ought to hold it down with safety pins. We will have lunch together if she ever comes. We should have gone jogging. Maybe that's why shes gotten thin, and I haven't. I never did like exercise. I hate doing something with my feet when I could be doing something with my head. "We should always be grateful," my mother says, "like in the Bible, happy with what were given." That's funny coming from my mother who isn't happy with anything in her life, including me. Laurie's mother wasn't keen on her, either. Maybe that's why we got along so well, two stranglings. Two nerds. Smart, but how far will smart get you?

That Laurie would be late was one thing you could count on. Why is it you can count on the bad things happening more than the good? Ah, here comes Laurie, look at that; she's wearing a

Black Diamond mink. Not politically correct, but stunning. Bet she won't say anything about not being here on time. She saunters in; she should have been here fifteen minutes ago. So true to form. No apology. Just, "Hello, Linda."

"Do you think I should wear this coat tonight to our re-union?" she asks as she sits down. "Maybe its too much. Milt says forget it."

She is slender as a knitting needle, a bony, angular, gauntness that guards her boney heart. She sits down gingerly as though she is having some kind of back pain and throws her coat onto an empty chair. "When did you get that?" I ask. "I never knew you had a mink."

"It's not mine."

I notice someone else's initials embroidered on the silk lining.

"Milt would never spring for a mink. No, Gladys lent it to me, it was her idea. Its kind of a kick."

"I wish I had a friend to lend me a coat like that, "I say.

"It's too fancy. Makes me look bad by contrast," she says.

Laurie was not plain; she had always been attractive, green eyes the color of seaweed, shining black hair worn waist length. Me, I was the *meiskite,* not her. My hair doesn't hold the curl; its always drooping in rainy weather. I have started to have brown spots, the evil form of the freckle. I always used to think of myself as an ungainly, misbegotten thing. I remember what my mother said when I told her I wanted to get an MBA. What do you think a *meiskite* like you is going to do with a business degree? Get a job, get married and you don't have to worry about a degree.

My mother was from some place deep in Russia, had come here as a young girl, never got past grade school. She always wore a scarf around her head, winter or summer, the same black scarf. She was not in favor of education for girls, but she was in favor of money; we always needed money because my dad had died when I was little, and my mom didn't make much as a seamstress.

I didn't have as bad a time in high school as Laurie; I accepted I would never be beautiful, or be in the in crowd. It hurts a lot less when you accept things, rather than fight against them. Fighting raises hope, like delicate spring seedlings. Expectations flourish and grow large, watered by imagination, and all that happens is a big old plant dies, not just a rude seedling. So I thought my salvation would be to leave home, go downstate to the University of Illinois. There was my hope spread out, like a sheet on an ironing board, and my mother crushed the idea, balled it up and threw it away. She wanted to keep me tied to her, a good work horse who could get a job and bring in a paycheck. Well, I can hardly blame her. Now that I think back about it, mother was frantic for money. It was a tune she sang under her breath, a tune without words, but a song heard, nevertheless. We never had enough. I never had enough.

I didn't like thinking about those times, yet here I was taking them out of their dark jackets, untying knotted strings, and planning to attend our high school reunion with Laurie and her husband. Neither she nor Milt had attended any reunion in forty years, although I had gone to a few of them. I was glad to slam the door on the past; she was ready to open it.

Our luncheon order arrives, and Laurie says, "Why do I need to put myself through this? The Delta Phi blackballed me, and

I'm sure Trish Keller will be there. I can't face her. She cast the deciding vote."

So, that was why Laurie had never attended a high school reunion. She was still a prisoner to Trish. In high school, Trish Keller had worn a thrusting bra that shaped her breasts like bullet-shaped Cadillac bumpers. Every boy claimed he had touched them. "How you found out who blackballed you, is beyond me." The scuttlebutt was she the only one who blackballed Davida Sturman, so she got in anyway. I'm sure she wouldn't be carrying around a thing like that for forty years, for heaven sakes. Davida and Trish had been the two most beautiful girls in our high school, worthy of my hatred.

Laurie puts on her bifocals to read the menu, orders iced tea to start. "Milt and I have been married for thirty years and while I was walking here, I wondered how it would be to do it with someone who had a bigger one. How would it feel?"

Wouldn't you know she'd bring up something like this. Always talking about her Milt this and her Milt that. Just to rub in that I'm divorced, she has to mention her Milt before she's even seen the menu. We both order something light, a salad, and iced tea.

"Big is an advantage," I agree and I don't say what I want to say. "Don't do me favors," I want to say. I shift the shopping bags on the floor between my ankles. My purse strap is firmly planted under one of her chair's legs. That way if someone tries to grab my bag, he'll have to take me, the purse, and the chair along with him. "It counts more who the man is than what size tool he's attached to." I see an opening to talk about Leonard.

Leonard is a big man, what I call stuffed. He is barrel-chested, his shirt is always in danger of bursting out of his jacket, his tie wants to strangle him. His arms dangle, stiff as clothespins, from his shoulders. When my husband beams his bright and shining intelligence on people, they fall back as though all their darkness is exposed. It made him a good lawyer, but it didn't gain him many friends.

"Leonard used sex as a way to get to sleep at night. Can you imagine, we were married for thirty-five years and the minute I left him he takes up with a little bitch who sucks up to him with a 'Gee you're wonderful, Leonard.' And she smiles with her newly minted teeth, 'Gee, Leonard, you're terrific.' By me he was never so terrific. What do you think Mr. Wonderful gave his new girl friend? A diamond pin. The diamonds are so small you could put them in your eye, but they're real. Her he gave diamonds; me he gave coal."

"How do you know this?" Laurie asks, cautious lest the spotlight slip off her. She sips her iced tea slowly.

"He told me, of course. He wants me to know how angry he is that I left him, a big-time attorney. He's furious that while we were still married I went back to school and finished my MBA on his money."

"I gotta give you credit for finishing your degree, standing up for yourself. And going by yourself to the reunion this evening. It's not an easy thing to do," says Laurie, taking papers out of her purse. "I think King is coming alone tonight, too," she adds as an afterthought, casual, like I wouldn't be interested, but secretly a little hope flourishes.

King (Jerry Seger's nickname in high school), held two letters in athletics, had been president of the Letterman's Club, charter member of the group that ruled by divine right. In actuality, of course, the circle of the disenfranchised was much larger than that of the privileged, but I didn't know it. All I knew was that, like most girls, I had a huge crush on the King of the school.

The gang knew that Jerry's family wasn't well off. Jerry dressed like everyone, even had an old car, but as money can smell money, money can smell when there is none. Throughout high school, King and Davida Sturman had been an item, but immediately upon graduation, they had been surgically separated by Davida's mother, who convinced her daughter to marry a different man, a very wealthy one. Eventually, Davida's husband lost most of his money in the stock market, while King, with the nerve of the street smart, made millions in real estate.

So Davida folded her hopes, like a Chinese fan, and remained the wife of a bald, short guy who, like her, remembered rather than lived his dreams. King married Adele Winter who had died just six months ago from breast cancer.

❏

When you're with people you haven't seen for a long time, the connection between the two of you remains forged, bolstered by the old familiarities and the newness of the moment. Sometimes, you want to get away as soon as possible. So it is with Laurie. I am ready to pay my half of the bill and leave, but before I can do so, she hands me a few sheets of paper.

"Here, look, this is what I plan to do on the program, but I'm nervous about it."

I look at the two typewritten pages. "You used to write a column for the school newspaper, but I never knew you wrote poems."

Laurie's frizzy dark hair springs out from her head in spiral curls. Her oval face contains hazel eyes and generous, heart-shaped lips. From a distance her skin is smooth, but up close, lines surge across her eyes, forehead, and the lower part of her face.

"Mac told me you faxed him the words, and boom, you were in. He really should have talked to me first. Not that I wouldn't have voted for you to be on the program, but I should have been consulted," I say, trying not to show I'm hurt. I had volunteered to be on the committee so I would have something to talk to people about at the reunion itself. It also gave me a good chance to catch up on the gossip. Mac Evans was the Chairman, and I was the co-chairman.

She is not exactly doing a poem, she explains, it is a rap without music. She had tried to memorize it, but no matter how much she practiced, she always ended up leaving something out.

She wears a beige dress with large white flowers sprinkled on it, two strands of fake pearls, not really in fashion, but not exactly out, and gold earrings. Laurie's lipstick never adheres to water glasses or linen napkins.

I read some of her song:

When I look in the mirror and I see those lines,
   Then I turn around — cellulite behind.
So I dye my hair, try to suck in my fat
   But forty years ago —
    I was just like that!"

Didn't have Sadam, Gorby or Nixon.
  Only high school kids played dirty tricks'n
  We had Jack Benny, Kuklah, Ollie and Fran,
    We had Prince Albert in the can.

"What do you think?" she asks. "Do you think they'll like it?"

"Of course," I say, "It's a good idea. You'll be the highlight of the evening." I was trying to be kind.

"What about the mink? Should I wear the mink?" she asks.

I try to reassure her. "Nobody cares if you have a mink."

"I never had cashmere sweaters like the Delta Phi. They were symbols, like today the kids want hundred dollar gym shoes. I just want to belong, that's all. Maybe it doesn't seem important to you, but I always felt invisible in high school."

"I wasn't any more popular than you."

We were on the outer fringes of everything. We were the nerds. Gawky. Gooky. Ugly.

I say, "Well, you're not awkward, icky, gawky or gooky now. So, forget about the mink. I don't like the idea of killing animals for pleasure."

"Oh, please. The Delta Phis love to kill whether it walks on two feet or four feet. I want to look good, I want to have what they have, or at least make them think I have what they have. I know it sounds childish, but once I change how they see me in the present, I can change how they saw me in the past."

"In the first place, you do have what they have. Isn't that true? Nice home, husband, kids. You could buy a mink if you wanted to."

"Don't you see, I need a status symbol so their image of me in the past will change." Laurie flashes me a sad look.

"I don't follow that one at all," I say.

"Well, you know people want to keep their image of you as you are, regardless of whether or not they like those qualities. It's like when someone fat loses weight, we start stuffing them with food, to keep them as they once were. When someone changes, we have to get used to them all over again. Change is scary. We prefer the devil we know to the devil we don't."

"Laurie, how can you go back in time to change that idea? Something that's done is done. It's impossible. You cant go back two minutes, much less forty years. When I did something stupid, it just stayed with me and probably the people I affected. You can't undo what's done, you can't unring a bell."

"Yes, but you could undo what the ring of that bell meant."

"You're talking bullshit. How in the world could you change how someone felt about you in the past?"

"If you read about some geeky kid you knew in high school who discovered the cure for cancer, you'd say, 'yeah, I always knew he could do it.' If a quiet kid becomes a criminal, you'd say, 'I knew he'd run into trouble.' Even though you never thought that, you tell yourself that you did because its hard to reconcile the new person with your idea of them in the past. There's a discrepancy between the old and new image, and we want to resolve the tension that discrepancy causes us to feel. And in trying to justify the old with the new, you alter that picture of the person that you had in the past to fit the new version."

"That sounds pretty Orwellian to me," I say.

❑

I arrive that night alone at the reunion. The Drexler hotel squats big on its city block, feeding on airport energy. Just behind me comes Milt, and Laurie wrapped in the Gladys mink. She wears it like shining armor, $30,000 worth of invincibility, the price of two years tuition at a fairly good college, but at the moment of her grand entrance into the cloakroom, no one is there but me. I feel sorry for her. She had counted on this moment so much.

"God listens to you, even what you leave out," Laurie says as she gives the cloakroom attendant the coat. "I should have prayed someone would be around when I took this off."

I understand her disappointment that no one was here to see the mink. Neither Laurie nor I had a mouton coat in high school. I remember Laurie's mother saying, "Persian lamb, mouton lamb, what's the difference? It's all lamb chops to me."

Laurie whispers a few lines from her song in my ear:

> *That mouton coat, can't forget it for a minute,*
> *When it got wet — smelled like*
> *The sheep were still in it.*

She goes over some more of the words with me, and I feel there's something wrong with her approach. The song makes fun of her and the audience as they were in high school. It's bright and cute, but discounting. I don't know how to tell her this and before I can say anything, a new surge of people enters the cloakroom, and sweeps us up into the State Street Ballroom. The ballroom has wall-to-wall beveled mirrors, and heavy gold drapes with deep swags over the high, elegant French windows. The floor is carpeted in a floral tapestry, and every thing around us looks new and polished. The singles and non-graduate spouses huddle around the bar for strength, while the alumni search for familiar faces. Then King wanders in. In high school he had been long and lean, a little over six feet tall. Now, possibly because he has put on a little weight, and his hair is almost all grey, King had more earthly characteristics. Then, as now, King never needed to introduce himself because people always knew who he was and sought him out. Whenever he met someone, the person making the introductions would say, "This is Jerry Seger." And the one being presented would invariably say, in a reverential voice, "Ah, yes. King, isn't it?"

Mr. Greshom, a World War II veteran, well into his seventies, makes his way toward a table and sits down. He is the only teacher the committee could find who was coherent, and interested in coming to the reunion. He was reputed to have a metal plate in his head that resonated to loud sounds. His chemistry class had been on the first floor of Theodore Craft High School, and whenever a fire truck went by, Mr. Greshom became agitated, rose from his seat with an odd look in his eye, and closed the window. It was not the sound of the fire truck that bothered Mr. Greshom, it was the rumbling it set up in his head.

Randolf Morrison, one of the alumni, waddles over to Laurie with a deferential air, as though apologizing in advance for any stupid acts he might inadvertently commit. Milt smiles and says hello, studying the high school annual picture of Randolf on his lapel card. Then, Randolf was a handsome young man, but now his face is drowning in a pool of fat. Laurie had a crush on Randolf in the old days, but I see she by the way she surveys the room as Randolf tries to engage her, that she wants nothing to do with him. We talk a while, then Randolf moves on.

The power brokers of the group do not rush over to meet anyone, but stand their ground at the bar, sipping drinks, knowing that eventually everyone would come to them. Laurie and Milt move away from Randolf. Tony Loma says hello to me, then walks up to the bar. I run to find Laurie.

"I can't believe that's Tony; he hasn't changed at all! Same shiny suit! Same Mafia tie. Same hair even, still greasy looking. And look, Alan Muckridge just came in with his wife. My God, I hardly recognize him. He's a body builder, not that squeaky little kid Tony used to beat up."

Laurie says in a low voice, "King is here, alone. What a shame about him and Davida. You know she's never come to one reunion, but I think he keeps hoping."

The band is playing Golden Oldies while the crowd looks for dinner table assignments. As luck would have it, Tony Loma, Alan Muckridge and his wife, Tina, sit at the same table with me, along with Laurie, her husband, and the Aron twins. There is an empty seat, deep red velvet, between Alan and Tony Loma, creating a kind of buffer zone.

"Someone didn't have the nerve to come," says Laurie and puts her handbag on the empty chair. She turns to Alan and asks about Fred Wangle, who has not shown up.

"You mean Lo-Ball?" asks Alan. "He's a dentist out in Jersey. Last time I saw him, he looked like an old man. Nobody would recognize him."

Tony turns to Alan, "Say, I know you. Aren't you Sydney Sweetzer, the big TV writer?"

Alan and Tina turn toward Tony. "No, I'm Alan Muckridge. You're thinking about Daryll Dickman. He's the writer."

Tony says, "You mean Daryll *Dickhead* Dickman? The guy who had warts on it? He was pals with Iggy Zits."

"Iggy Zits? Did you ever call him that to his face?" Alan's biceps twitch under his jacket.

Tony laughs. "Iggy had warts on his ass, never washed his gym shorts."

"Will you guys cut it out with the warts," says Laurie.

Tony says,"That reminds me of Dina Wartsky."

"I think you mean Tina Bresky," I jump in.

Tony says to Alan, "The one with the humongus honkers? "

Tina is sitting at her husbands side, and her ears perk up. Tony keeps on talking, not understanding that Tina is there.

"She sure put out for a lot of guys. Say, you're a big guy. She ever put out for you?"

"No, not then."

"When then?" Tony will not let up.

Alan struggles to maintain his composure, I see his hand pulling down on his wife's shoulder as she struggles to rise. A cup of hot coffee is in her hand. I'm pretty sure I know what she is going to do; strange that Tony Loma doesn't.

"Later on, when we got married," Alan says in a fierce whisper. Alan stands and pulls Tony Loma up by the lapels. Whatever he was going to say is interrupted by a waiter serving a fully inflated chocolate mousse. Tina's hand shakes as she holds her coffee cup; coffee sloshes about. The waiter bends over to serve dessert and blocks her aim so she sits down, eyes shining bright ready to search and destroy.

❑

I see Trish Keller at another table, still gorgeous, breasts thrust out like medals. Her eyes are the kind of crystalline blue that makes you think of summer skies and honeybees. She sits in kind of a blonde cloud, remote as ever and still beautiful. Noreen Lundell walks by her table, and I see Trish wince. Noreen, has the face of a fox terrier, and was the terror of our school. She had a big sassy mouth, always found a person's weak points and picked at them. If she didn't like you, she'd kick in your gym locker. There were a lot of lockers kicked in at Theodore Craft. Mine was one of them.

Laurie excuses herself, and when she returns from the ladies' room has a note of hysteria in her voice. She whispers, "No notes. I cant find my notes. What am I going to do?" She was sure she had brought them. Now she's got to do the song from memory, and she has been unable to memorize it. I feel sorry for her; the moment she thought would change history would just confirm it. Laurie's face is white, she feels sick.

Mac begins the program with a tribute to our teachers, and Mr. Greshom stands up, trembling on his cane, to be recognized. I remember that in our chemistry class Noreen Lundell had egged the Aaron twins on to urinate into Randolf Morrison's chemistry experiment, and the results of whatever he was testing never did come out right. "Too much sugar." Greshom had said, looking at Randolf in a strange way, as though expecting Randolf to know precisely what liquid was in the glass beaker. "Too much sugar."

"Sugar, sir?" poor Randolf said. "Sugar?"

From that day on Greshom terrorized Randolf, making him recite the symbols of every element from memory, called on him for every calculation, teased him at every turn. Randolf forced down his anger and humiliation and tried to get on with his life, but every now and then when Noreen was feeling especially vindictive, she'd mumble under her breath, "Sugar," just loudly enough so Randolf could hear it.

Laurie comes on stage to do her part. She is shaking. "I faxed Mac the words to my song," she says. "And he's the kind of guy you'd like to fax more than once." The audience perks up and starts to listen. "I was going to do a rap song, but I'm afraid I can't find my notes. It wasn't a great song, so maybe it's no great loss. I just thought I'd like to reminisce for a few minutes about our high school days, since I haven't seen most of you in almost forty years. "

She starts out slow, being embarrassed about not doing her song, but as she speaks about our school days, how insecure she was, how sad the school now looks with graffiti all over the building, she touches almost everyone; the "ins" as well as the "outs." She even mentions, much to Noreen's embarrassment, how Noreen used to kick in gym lockers, and the audience laughs in forgiveness. Laurie finishes, the audience claps. Then suddenly she adds that we should all get together and put some money in a fund to help clean up the old school building, so our memories can stay bright and shining, and people dig down in their pockets, pull out checkbooks, and make donations on the spot. She collects almost a thousand dollars. I can't say if she changed anyone else's opinion of her, but I know I she changed mine.

❑

I sit at the table alone. Everyone else is dancing. I figure this would be a good time to go to the ladies' room. Suddenly, I see King coming slowly toward me. In my mind's eye I see him as he once was—young, wavy dark hair, wearing his scarlet and blue letterman's jacket. The handsomest boy in class. There is a spring to his gait as he comes and sits next to me on a velvet chair.

"Hi," he says. "Remember me? I'm Jerry."

Of course I remember him. What woman wouldn't? What a difference between him and my ex. My ex likes to rub in how great his new girl friend is. I hate her boney bones. Size six, he also let me know that. She has trouble gaining weight. She can't be Jewish. As soon as we separated, the casserole brigade began. Ladies toting crock pots with something simmering, flocking down on him. Beware of women bearing hot dishes, like Trojan horses, there's something else inside.

"You look great," King says.

"You too. Seems hard to believe we're all in our fifties. The only way I qualify as a younger woman is to go out with a man of ninety."

Jerry laughs. "You're divorced?"

"News travels fast."

"If you want it to."

"And you?"

"Adele is gone." He says no more.

"Yes, I heard, I'm sorry."

"How about a dance?" he says. "They're playing one of the few things I can dance to."

We get on the floor. Noreen is dancing with Randolf. The girl who was the terror of our school does not look intimidating anymore. She is just a grey-haired woman with cracks skipping along the top of her lips, wearing a high collar to hide her crepey neck.

Jerry asks questions about me and Leonard. I don't tell him how tight with a dollar Leonard was. That I had to account for every penny, that he went berserk if I didn't buy on sale. I bought forty dollar shoes for twenty-five and I say, "Guess how much I paid."

And he says, "Fifteen dollars would be too much."

I don't tell him because I know how men identify with each other, how they hate to spend. Anyway, men don't want to hear your old problems. They're too busy trying to tell you theirs.

Jerry holds me tight; we dance to a bunch of old tunes. He starts talking to me about his life and occasionally I say, "uhm," and he skates on. It's easy to keep men talking once they start.

I am not thinking about him, but of my old life. I didn't tell him how my mother always called me a *meiskite* and Leonard took over from there. And I wore size eight then. I starved myself because Leonard said that he didn't want to be married to a fat cow. When I look back at my old pictures, I see I was pretty nice looking, I had dimples, beautiful long hair, a lovely smile. It breaks my heart to look back at my old photographs and see how I pretty I was when I thought I was ugly.

The band takes a break. Jerry continues to talk about himself. How in high school he worked at a gas station on the other side of town so no one would know he needed to earn pocket money. How stupid he felt because he never understood geometry, or calculus. How his grades weren't good enough to get him into college. How he really hadn't gotten over the death of his wife, Adele, and how lost he feels without her. I stop thinking about myself and listen to him, especially the things he doesn't say. He says nothing at all about Davida, but she hovers over the reunion. An unacknowledged ghost.

❑

The band comes back and we dance again to something old, something smooth. Its the kind of music you can talk over. I tell Jerry he doesn't have to spend all his time with me, there probably are a lot of people he'd like to talk to, and who would like to see him. "No one that really matters," he says, and we keep on dancing. He tells me about his kids and his new grandchild. He asks how I met Leonard.

I can smell Jerry's aftershave, something pine, something of salt and a touch of ash. I tell him I was wearing a new dress when I first met Leonard. On sale of course. But it was red and flashy with a boat neckline, and I felt like a firecracker in it.

"I always thought of you that way," he says.

"Really, you thought I was a firecracker? That was certainly not my perception of myself in high school."

Now he says, "Uhm," and I let it go at that. Jerry just holds me tighter. The music flows, mellow as scotch. I could have said more, could have told him that my mom said, What are you buying? New dress? New shoes? Always something. My mother hated Leonard instantly. That was enough for me; anything she detested, I liked, and we married a few months later.

❑

The band plays on. They're playing, *Come On to My House* with Rosemary Clooney, a popular song at the time I was six months pregnant living in a third floor walk-up near Hyde Park High School on the south side of Chicago.

I longed for watermelons. When you live in a third floor walk-up, you eat grapes, and apples and berries. That's stair fruit, the little stuff. Schlepping up watermelons was too heavy for me. Still I dragged the groceries to the third floor, and sometimes even seltzer, and the parts for the crib. One day, I was visiting Mom and I felt a tightening and a pain. I cried to my mom and she said to me, in Yiddish, "You American girls have it too easy." I called my doctor who told me to stay in bed and not get up. When I laid down on my mother's couch she said to the air, "These poor American girls, they're such prima donas."

When Leonard came he drove me to the doctor's office and the doctor told us to go straight to the hospital. I was dilated and it looked like I was going to abort. I was so scared. He said the chances were slim that the baby would live, and it would probably be better if it didn't. It probably wouldn't be normal. Those were the days before ultrasound and all that fancy stuff they do now. We would have to wait and see.

Leonard said if the baby wasn't right, it was better off not living. I wanted it to live no matter what. But I had little chance to think about it because I went into labor almost immediately. I delivered a girl. Perfect in every way except she was dead.

Leonard said that she was a strange maroon color. The doctor told him that was typical in premature babies.

This year she would be twenty-two. They didn't want me to see her, they never showed her to me. Who was I to ask? To question the doctors, to tell Leonard I wanted to see her. He had already written off her existence.

"You'll have another," my doctor told me. My mother came to the hospital and said the same thing, but that didn't help me.

I did get pregnant again, but of course, no baby can replace another. I still mourn for her, I dream for her, the girl that might have been. And what did my mother say? She said it was better this way. The baby was a *meiskite*.

These are the thoughts in my head as I'm dancing and they go by in a flash, like events in a dream that lasts only a few seconds but feels like more. Isn't that like life itself? We try to catch it in a net and it eludes us. It flutters beyond our reach and we fall back to earth never understanding what it all meant.

"What are you thinking about? "says Jerry. The dance is over.

"Nothing much," I say.

❑

The photographer announces he is ready to take the alumni photograph. As the graduates begin to make their way toward the stage where the photographer is set up, Trish Keller comes up to congratulate Laurie on her performance.

"I can't believe what you said that about Noreen kicking in your locker," she says. "That woman used to terrorize me; you wouldn't believe how many times I cried about Noreen in therapy."

"Noreen? Noreen bothered you?" Laurie says, looking at the lovely woman with tears in her eyes; one of the chosen inner circle.

"Noreen had it in for me. She made my life miserable. She kicked in my locker and frightened me to death for four years. She threatened to beat me up after school." Trish blows into her hankie. "I'll be OK," she said.

Laurie looks hard at the woman she had always admired and hated. "But you were in Delta Phi. I always thought you had everything!"

"Delta Phi?" Trish laughed bitterly. "There was a pecking order in Delta Phi, you know. Davida was on top. Everyone else was second best. Davida tried to keep me out of the sorority, because she knew I liked King and Noreen hated me for no reason at all. I'm glad those days are over now, and it's just as well."

"I'm sorry those people were mean to you," Laurie says, clasping Trish's hand, as they walk to the rear of the room. The photographer is just about to take the reunion photograph. The graduates stand in formation on long benches. I run down the aisle and Laurie yells for the photographer to wait for us.

Randolf Morrison waves to us from the top step, "Come on, come on."

"Wait for us," Laurie calls, and to our complete astonishment, they do.

Mr. Greshom, is next to Randolf, mumbling a word under his breath that sounds suspiciously like "sugar." The Aron twins, alike as teeth, are in the back row. Tony and Alan flank the sides of the photograph, standing as far away from each other as possible.

Alan grasps Laurie's hand, almost lifting her out of her high heels, and makes all the bald heads in front of her hunker down so that her face might be seen. Jerry Seger, already established at the center of the photo pulls me up by the wrist to join him. I remember taking our graduation photo, forty years ago. How Tony Loma had put up a crude sign with two fingers in back of someone's head and how we had to take the picture over again. We were young then, dreaming of growing up. Now we are old, dreaming of our youth. We cannot take this picture again. So many things that were important drifted beyond the reach of our nets. Then, Laurie and I had felt like outsiders but now we were gathered in.

"Smile," said the photographer. And we did.

❏

My Husband Asked,
"What Did You Do Today, Dear"

I tied six shoes twenty times for three persons
    Under seven.
  Poured sand out of same shoes twenty-one times.
Washed half the baby, bottom half.
  Diapered her eight times and
  Felt guilty for not checking her more often.
  Laundered two sets of wee-weed sheets.
Prepared five burned to a crisp
    Cheese sandwiches and threw all away
    Because children wouldn't eat them.
I hadn't meant to incinerate them.
    At most, just toast but I looked away
    For just a moment.
They wouldn't eat the replacement French toast
    Which was also burnt.
I put dishwashing detergent in the dishwasher.
    A mistake.
The knob came off the bathroom door locking me OUT
    And them IN.
Bottles of cranberry juice jumped out of the paper bag
    And broke on my kitchen floor.
    It used to be white.
The oldest child fell on the canary when
    It flew out of its cage and landed on the floor.
Two children jumped off the dresser
    Because it was there.
 Well, that was my day. How was yours?

Happy Anniversary

I guess I'm in love with you.
We've been sleeping together for twenty years,
And I'm just about resigned
To wearing ear plugs when you snore
Instead of kicking you awake.
I watch you brushing your teeth,
Smelling up the bathroom,
Leaving all those chopped-up hairs in the sink,
Which I must clean up or watch rise
Like a spider come to life.
I sort piles of indistinguishable black socks
And use your old tee shirts for rags.

We sometimes miss each other
Even when we're in the same room,
But mostly we shout.
I cry.
You keep yourself in a black brief-case,
You tote it to work every day,
Where you do unexplainable things that
Keep us in orthodontia, ballet lessons and
Gummed reinforcements.

Our life of odds and ends stitches a life quilt
To warm us when we are old and cold.
We swam through a soggy zwieback sea together.
I'm reminding you three weeks ahead of time
About our coming anniversary in case
You had any special shopping to do.
I want you to know I thought enough
To send the very best.
Me.

Happy Anniversary.

❑

e Recipe

eserve a Husband

Be careful not to choose one too young or green,

Or those that have not been raised
  in a proper environment.

The best kinds are firm but yielding to the touch.

To prepare for domestic use,

Never keep them in a pickle or hot water

Or salt them or put them in dark places

Where they might rot.

This only makes them sour, hard and bitter.

Even poor varieties may become sweet and tender

By garnishing them with patience,

Well-seasoned with smiles and flavored
  with kisses to taste.

To prepare, instead of cutting off the rough spots,

Wrap them carefully in understanding,

Keep them warm with a steady fire

And don't let them boil over while simmering.

Best served with peaches and cream.

When properly prepared, they will keep for years.

❑

Little Old Ladies

Little old ladies before me in lines
At the supermarket,
Drift slowly down the aisle like stray puffs
Of smoke,
Sag wearily at the check-out counter.
"Hello, Ed," they say, reading
The bag-boy's name tag.
He does not know theirs.

They count their money as though surprised
How little there is.
Put back the strawberries,
Ask for subtotals, wonder if they have
Enough to pay.

Little old ladies before me in lines
At the lingerie counter,
Moving like frail dreamers,
Fingering the nightgowns,
Tracing lace patterns with worn fingertips.

The saleslady condescends,
"May I help you?"
"Just looking," they say in papery voices,
And soon shrink away.

Little old ladies before me in lines
Waiting to grunt up the steps of the bus with
Quarters and dimes.
Marking time with their canes,
Patiently waiting
Until I become one of them.

Little old ladies before me in lines
Bunching together like nervous birds for walks
In the park and lunch.
They never go out after dark.
Shaking and palsied, limping and lame.

Dear ladies, where are all your little old men?

❑

Los Angeles

Crazy freak.
Weird, Gaudy, Plastic.
Bright with fear. Black widow feeding on her mate.
Night flowering creature
Sporting diamonds on a tacky dress.
Forgotten lines, remembered lies.

Cameras grind the scene;
Hills frizzed with brush.
Citrus trees transmogrified into
Orange Julius.

Babys toes, black Cayolas,
Root beer,
Worn out graffiti.
Predictable sex and wet spots.

Cities hard with frozen neon.
Too bright, lighting faces
We'd rather not see.
Pastel encounters. Primitive dreams.
Smog cataracts.
Imperfect vision between graces,
Thwarted Bird of Paradise.

❏

LA Riots

Ever since the riots, the air has the smell of fried dreams
And burning paint, charred blackness
That descends in the early afternoon.
Ever since the riots, the smell of gasoline floats
Like a gray winter rain that scrapes our raw skin.

The odor of defeat and anguish and motorcycle cops
And television sets ripped out through windows,
Cracked and crazed like spider webs.
Mothers with their kids helped themselves
Just like they were taking seconds at Sunday dinner.

Anchor mens striped ties, and crackling papers tell us
That white smoke is better than black.
Black means something's burning,
White means nothing's left.
Fear stings our eyes.

In South central there is the smell of wet clothes,
Rotting fish, damp newspapers, vacuum tubes
And everything connected by wires.
The smell of coleslaw, lock jaw and bullets, lard
And fried things three days old.
Stale water, bug , bad breath.

That was the day our dreams got fried.

❑

Machine Gun Shoes

DELANEY STUDIES THE PHOTOGRAPHS OF PEOPLE WITH HARELIPS and wonders how she would look if she had been born that way. Mother doesn't like her reading father's medical books, but the pictures of boils and crippled bodies and the names of diseases are fascinating. She loves to curl the words around in her mouth; "hyperthyroidism," "hypothyroidism," "hypochondria," "hysteria." And that's only the h's.

She puts the volume she had been reading back in its place on the book shelf. Father has no tolerance for disorder. Once assigned, everything must stay in place. Everything that has no place must be given one. Twenty-four hours are too long for limbo, twenty-four minutes unbearable. Things must be classified in twenty-four seconds, put where they are supposed to go, locked up and not moved except when dusted.

Lace curtains drape the windows in her father's study, keep the sun from scalding the room. A clear plastic statue of a man without skin sits on the scarred mahogany desk. His arteries are red, veins blue, his muscles look like uncooked pot roasts. Next to him is a bottle of ink, like the color of the sea at midnight. Delaney likes to make ink blots similar to the ones she sees in the text books. She takes a piece of typing paper from the drawer near the L.C. Smith typewriter, creases it, drops a blob from the ink well in the middle of the ridge, then folds the paper in half and smooths out designs that look like butterflies with the heads of snakes and grinning mouths without faces.

Her father's pipe lies on the desk. There is an acrid off-center smell in the blackened bowl, like the insides of rotting tree stumps. Next to the pipe is a white box of Lucky Strikes. She vaguely remembers the package used to be green. The old slogan was "LSMFT", "Lucky Strike Means Fine Tobacco," but the new slogan is "Lucky Strike Green Has Gone to War." Her father told her that the green color from the old boxes is now being used to dye soldier's uniforms.

Delaney and her friends know there is fighting "over there," but they fear someday World War II will be here, in Denver. The mountains will not be able to protect them and bombers will come down Colfax Street. Children will hide where they can, cradle their heads with their arms, and try not to pee..

She is afraid something bad will happen. She thinks in a strange, dismembered jumble of images; a certain liturgy of words, Bataan, Corregidor, War Bonds and Gold Star Mothers who made an offering to the appetite of war. Fear is secreted in her body, layer upon layer of dread wrapping a black pearl in the pit of her stomach, and every week, with the showing of Fox Movie Tone News, the pearl at the bottom of her stomach grows larger.

Once, she and her parents took the train from Union Station to Colorado Springs and she saw squads of soldiers in transit. They flowed around her, all identical in khaki, Adam's apples, strange caps that cut against the grain of their hair, eyes that had not yet learned to turn inward, and all she could think of was whether or not there was any green dye in their uniforms.

Delaney turns her attention to her mother and father's wedding picture sitting next to the half-empty cigarette box. Mother stiffly holds an undernourished floral bouquet of trailing roses. Her face is stamped with the same anxiety Delaney feels. She is young and slight with a smile that looks like she was forced to hold on to it too long. Her father is encased in a military uniform, no older than the soldiers at Union Station.

Her parents met when Grandpa gave his daughter's name to a matchmaker without her knowledge and arranged for the trembling lieutenant to come to dinner. When her father or Grandma tells the story, her mother remains quiet.

"Surely, you had free choice, didn't you, Mama?" Delaney once asked when they were alone. She sought to befriend her mother as only a daughter could, afraid and yet in some secret way, eager to hear the confession.

"There were reasons," was all mother would say. Her future was packed up in a suitcase by her parents and she was sent on her way.

Delaney feels sorry for her mother, and yet views her with contempt. She will not be so compliant when she grows up. She will look like Wonder Woman if she looses weight, she will wear metal bracelets that stop bullets, she will live on an isle of Amazon women who rule themselves without men.

"What are you doing, Lovey?" Mother's voice pricks her skin like thumbtacks. It is sparse, asymmetrical, overly sweetened. Removed. She always uses that vague, unfocused high pitch to call Delaney from whatever minor pleasures she might have.

Mother's eyes are the color of toasted almonds, her clear light skin is stretched tightly over her face. She wears a floral patterned blue house dress, and an embroidered apron with food stains that begin at the waist and go down the full length of the apron.

"Lovey?" Mother calls again. Delaney has put on the headphone of her radio. It is a crystal set she made from a kit, but her mother's voice can still be heard. "I swear," Mother says loud enough for Delaney to hear, "I don't know what an eleven year old girl would want with those books. Put them back and come in here."

The air is hot, condensed, compacted, forced into her father's study and held against its will. Delaney moves the stylus called a cat's whisker, to a different place on the crystal so she can hear better, holds the ear piece closer. President Truman isn't sorry he used the bomb last year. He looks and sounds like Chick, the farmer who brings fresh eggs right up to their door once a week. Both men have gravel in their throats and a stubborn set to the jaw that says they are not men to be rushed. She moves the stylus again, hoping to pick up "I Love A Mystery" or "Inner Sanctum" with Raymond Johnson Edwards, the host, and his creaking door. When she was younger, the rusty squeaking sent her shivering into the world of the unexplained.

She wanted to reproduce of that sound so she saved box tops from cereals and sent in for a sound effects set. It contained coconut shells for the sound of horses' hooves (rap on the table top), cellophane (crinkle) for the sound of fire, a wooden train whistle and a cardboard mike that fit on top of a broom handle, but no squeaking door.

Father says the programs are nonsense. He has the bearing of an opera singer and gives the impression of being taller than he is. He steps forward on the balls of his feet as though he is wearing elevator shoes, as though any moment he will grow taller and engulf her, or rise from the ground. There is an air preceding him that sends the message, "he's coming, he's coming." His patients watch out the window for his arrival. They have plenty of Maxwell House coffee ready and home made pies still warm from the oven. They hope he will grace them with his presence, and a cure.

Delaney's hair falls like thick steel chains from her head, dropping straight down without a kink or curl. She is wearing a pink Angora sweater and a pair of slacks with a safety pin holding them together. There is something thick and substantial about her body, a toughness of the flesh. She is tall for her age, always has to stand in the rear of a class photograph with the boys whose ears look ready to lurch off their heads at awkward angles. She sees over the tops of most girls, their bows and barrettes holding back braids with frizzy ends and curls that had been unwrapped just before breakfast. She prays someday to be short.

Delaney's mother calls again. It is the lost call of a goose, it is a scratching from within, it supposed to be kind, yet it comes out over-exposed, like photographs that bleed in the light. Delaney will be quiet in her father's study; after calling three times her mother usually gives up. But today, there is a note of urgency in mother's voice, a different tone that says if you don't come here right now, it will happen.

Livia, a white Angora cat, glides across father's desk with impunity, never knocking over the model of a human head from Merck, Sharp and Dohme, a pharmaceutical house. The skull comes off to reveal a brain the size of a baseball, pink as baby lips, that Delaney likes to take out and hold in the palm of her hand. Will doctors take her brain out someday? Hold it in their hands? See her thoughts as though on a movie screen? She shudders in as she traces the parts of the cerebral hemisphere her father has labeled in tiny, elegant letters; the corpus callosum, the occipital lobe, the magical sounding medulla oblongata.

The cat pushes itself into a claustrophobic space between a three dimensional model of an eye ball and a Lucite cube with a mouse embryo embedded in it. Delaney follows Livia to the kitchen wondering if Angora sweaters are made from cats.

Mother calls again. Mother wants help in the basement with the canning. All the fruit has to be rinsed off, gutted, prepared. There is a sweet smell in the room like honey, ants and decayed melons. Last winter the home-canned tomatoes exploded out of their Mason jars, followed a week later by peaches, and shortly after that, plum preserves sprayed the walls.

When the canning jars blasted off, it was the corner of the night where everything that could not stop made a left turn and unraveled. Delaney's breathing was slow and steady when suddenly there was an explosion downstairs followed by silence, then a series of thudding sounds in rapid succession, and silence again. Delaney jumped out of bed, wearing a faded pink night gown with a picture of Bambi on it and ran down the hall with mother and father a second behind. The cellar floor was livid with blobs of fruit interspersed with glass and pulp puree, the fragments crunched underfoot foot like Corn Flakes. Even though she hates to help clean up, she's grateful that at last something interesting is happening. Still, she wonders why all the preserves didn't blow up. They were all canned in the same batch, yet some of the peaches still strain against their bottle prisons, preternaturally yellowed, glowing in the deep recesses of the basement, falling back from the light like mushrooms.

She remembers her dad yelling at mother for allowing the canned goods to explode. "Botulism," he cried, "botulism. You'll kill us all!"

The next evening when father came home from hospital rounds, he made mother go over the list of ingredients and her canning process. She offered explanations, and he rejected them all. He wanted everything to be concentrated, fan-folded, filed away under solved. Mother was reduced to a tented silence, frowning into her wine glass. Delaney imagined that she was thinking about killing her husband with other home made desserts.

Delaney thinks the cans blow up because her mother has willed them to. Mother is depressed much of the time and takes medicines from the box in the closet to control what she calls nerves, so that nothing spills over in her.

Delaney craves the samples in the big Abbott Labs carton where her father throws them; vitamins, Phenobarbital, cough lozenges, nose drops, Seconal, iodine, Emperin, Gentian Violet. She contemplates the colors and sizes of the capsules, ruminates on their contents like an alchemist. The formula for Phenobarbital is $C12H12N2O3$. If you played around with the numbers, her father said, and took out the Nitrogen, you would get sugar, $C12H22O11$.

She takes Dexedrine because she is chunking up and wants to lose weight. The pills make her heart beat too fast and she feels as though she is breathing through her skin and the top of her head might come off like that model on the desk. And what would come out? Devious things with feet and hooded faces that could never be captured once they were free.

Yesterday Delaney tried out a new magic potion on her dolls. She doesn't play with them much anymore, uses them for experimental purposes only. She set them on pillows before a low wooden table. One is loosing her hair and has a terrible thyroid problem, another has a cracked eye and is going blind, the blue-eyed blonde with braids like Heidi has no underpants and needs immediate surgery. Delaney crushed ten aspirins, added a full bottle of nose drops, a touch of honey, two glasses of strong tea, cherry pits and a few capsules of Phenobarbital. She put it into her dolls' tea pot and carefully poured the liquid in little china cups with polite blue flowers on them. The tea set was a gift from Grandma when Grandma was fat. She poured slowly and placed a cup before each of her guests and whispered, "Don't die, dears."

Mother sits at the kitchen table slicing, holding a cigarette in one hand, an ash occasionally falling on the cutting board. She wipes the ash off the board, and rubs her hand with the bottom of her apron. She is drinking a glass of wine and asks her daughter to cut up the tomatoes. Although mother says it without a show of force, Delaney cooperates because the knife her mother holds is long and sharp.

She wishes she was wearing her imaginary shoes that look like machine guns. They have skyscraper heels made out of switch blades, ice picks, or syringes with deadly poison. The vamps of the shoes shoot bullets from their toes, the soles pull back and bombs drop out of them. Not only are the shoes lethal, they have the power to make her airborne so she can fly over her house on South High Street, where she see everything that's happening without being seen.

The houses are lined up waving hello with the day's wash, sheets flap against each other's backs, bleached by the sun and shot with an odor that can only be caught on the back of the tongue. Roofs incline towards the Rocky mountains, back yards have fruiting trees, and in the Spring, the air is cauterized with the aroma of lilies-of-the-valley and lilacs so intensely sweet you'd think they could be baked in a pie.

From the air she would be able to see the monster chow dog that lives next door, its tongue a garish purple color, her schoolmates playing hide and seek. If she was "it" this time, they wouldn't be able to find her because she would hide far up on a cloud. Then she would bomb them all with bombs from her shoes. Perhaps mother and dad will get hit by the bombs, preferably atomic.

She wonders why her mother cans food. In some vague way it is good for the war effort. There is a tin of rendered chicken fat in the refrigerator, it too is good for the fighting men. When the can is full, grandfather takes it to his butcher shop for red points that can be exchanged for meat rations. Delaney does not understand how bullets can be made from fat. She remembers the shop, Grandpa's wood handled carving knives, clean wood shavings on the floor that concealed drops of rust colored blood on the gray cement. He drinks beer in his undershirt in the summer, listening to baseball on the radio. No matter how hard she tried, she could not see the game in her mind like he did, yet she could clearly see the machine gun shoes in her head. Someday she will have a real pair.

She looks into her mother's eyes and sees a vacant field of brown with a orange ring around the iris. It is like looking into a long dark well, like scooping up air holes and resignation. In her eyes, Delaney sees the faces of cats who want to be fed, buttons unsewn, and the need to move on.

Sometimes Delaney lies on her parent's big double bed, wrapped in the mountains of a down comforter, watching her mother get dressed. She thinks her mother was born of a dragonfly, spit, ax blades and old candle wax. That she had risen from vapors, a cold plumaged bird with a tanzinite heart and corrosive hair.

Her mother came to the mirror as though its slick surface could be licked into submission. She would lay her cheek against the mirror, then back away and look at herself full face, then sigh and close her eyes. It was then that Delaney thought she saw something wriggling under the surface of her skin. Mother seemed to be searching for herself, but apparently found only an impostor.

First her mother would stand on the white octagon tiled bathroom floor and smear flesh colored makeup on her legs. When that dried, she would stand on the bed in front of the mirror and draw black lines up the back of her legs to give the impression of seamed nylon stockings. The line always came out crooked so her mother would have to rub it off and try again. Sometimes Delaney would try to make the stocking lines for her Mother, holding her lips tightly against each other as she drew the line past blue varicose veins that ran the from the back of the ankle to the knee, gnarled and thick as tree branches.

The last thing before putting on her dress, Mother would center herself inside a girdle and hook it shut. The corset was made of a vague pink thick material with embossed flowers on it, so light they could barely be seen and lined with vertical stays from the top to the bottom of the garment. Mother tugged at the laces hanging down on each side and pulled these until her waist became more narrow. Then she hooked a matching pink brassiere onto the foundation garment. It was like watching a horse being put into harness.

Sometimes Delaney would stand at the mirror and stare at the two of them in the trying to figure out which was the mother.

Her father, unlike her mother, came from an arcane medical planet, where everyone was born a doctor with a white laboratory coat tattooed on his body. He was wet nursed by a woman with milk the color of sunsets who spoke only Latin. He learned to read thermometer in Celsius, to tell the difference between the ileum and the ischium, and to only refer out under duress. Her father brags that there are seven doctors in his family whom he lists in descending order; one ophthalmologist, two chiropodists, one chiropractor, Uncle Nab the dog doctor and one Ph.D. who barely counted. Father says he is the only real physician among them.

There are three large bowls of tomatoes left on the table. With a look and no commentary, Mother tells Delaney to get back to work. Words have been torn out of her, stripped naked of meaning, unusable and homeless. Her words slither off each other like reptiles, to swim in deeper pools.

Delaney's juices simmer down. She is locked at this table until the tomatoes have been sliced.

Delaney's father comes home early from hospital rounds. He wears a gray felt hat, a dark suit with a feeble blue thread in it, a long sleeved white shirt still smelling of starch and sweat, and a tie the color of mud. Sometimes Delaney thinks the clothes themselves have come marching in without him. They sit right down for dinner and everyone pretends there is someone inside.

"You know I like to eat on time," he says. "I've got three house calls to make. Why didn't you pick up that paper in the living room? I left it there just to see if you'd notice." Mother doesn't have any answer, except to say that Delaney was no help at all. Grandma Kaye calls and Mother quickly hands over the phone to her husband, pours herself another glass of white wine from what looks like a bottle of refrigerated water. Delaney knows better.

Mother swears under her breath, "Ball-busting, harmonica-playing old biddy," she says of her mother-in-law and, cigarette still in hand, puts out food for Livia; and rubs its head.

Grandma used to be a bullet shaped woman whose waist was as big as her shoulders, a hulking presence with machine tooled hair, metallic frown, precisely dressed as though assembled by robots. Delaney remembers grandma moving squarely like a battle ship across the dining room floor, making the dishes in the china closet jump. Then, just six months ago, Grandma shrank. It was as though she had been wearing a huge fox coat, and took it off to reveal a completely different person inside — tiny, shriveled, condensed, looking something like a prune pit.

Her father puts the phone down, looks around the kitchen as though offended by the juicy, seedy pulp on the table.

"I can't sit there with all those damn tomatoes," Father says, "I just got out of surgery."

Delaney watches her mother's expressionless reaction, how she drops her eyes to look at the floor. Dad goes down the hall to his study and bangs the door. In her Xray vision Delaney can tell he's looking at the books, trying to detect if they were moved. Now her father will turn on Walter Winchell and listen and smoke Lucky Strike Green.

Something has fallen out of her mother, and she wonders if it will fall out of her, too. She tries to tell her girl friend Sheila, also eleven, that her Mother is purposely making the canned goods explode and that her mother wants to kill her.

Why would her mother kill her? Delaney isn't sure but it feels like mother wants something Delaney has. What could it be?

A few months ago, Delaney had opened the door to her parents' room and her mother was completely undressed in bed with her father. She had that dead light in her eyes. She was a slight woman, barely large enough to make a dent in the sheets. Mother snarled at her with a growl, then she fell back as though asleep. "Go out and play," her father said.

❑

They finish the tomatoes. Mother sits there in her flowered house dress, and apron with pert embroidered pansies in chef's hats. She wipes her dripping hands on her apron, stains the flowers red. She picks up the bowl full of tomatoes, carries them to the bathroom and flushes them down the toilet. "It's too much work," she says. Then she makes dinner.

Delaney goes out to climb the cherry tree. There are dots of lint in the air, the sky is scoured with sharp looking clouds and there is a hovering dry, sour scent born of the outgrown wings of bees, and leaves that have died from thirst, even though the neighbor boys have urinated on them. Summer will be leaving soon.

The whole back yard, bordered by a three foot high weathered wooden fence, centers around the cherry tree. Giant sunflowers taller than a man, grow wild towards the rear of the yard, tomatoes with crimson coats bend with the heaviness of their fruits, and sport horrible looking, spiky caterpillars. White and purple lilac trees spread their incense like a layer of fog. Everything dazzles as though it has just been polished.

Delaney loves to eat the tart Queen Anns, to climb to the highest tree branch where the ripest ones hide. She thinks about the metal instruments her father keeps in the sterilizer in his study and wonders what he uses them for. She is glad to get away from her mother who can sit still and silent as a department store mannequin. On a good day, her mother used to hum show tunes, but now mostly she's quiet.

The image of her mother flickers in Delaney's mind like water droplets from a garden spray. She's just a shadowy round shouldered image wearing a benign navy blue sweater winter and summer. Gray hair so fine it looks like lace on the top of her head. Sometimes Delaney, at night, trying to recall her mother's face, loses it.

Even though Delaney had taken Dexedrine only a few hours ago, she nibbles the cherries. It's a game she invented, trying to outwit the pills. She shouldn't be hungry, and she isn't, but she stuffs one cherry after another in her mouth and spits out the smooth pits after every bit of flesh has been sucked off.

After a dinner of brisket and home-made cherry pie, her father complains that the cherries are too tart, the pie should have had more sugar. Her mother just shrugs and throws away the remains on his plate and the rest of the pie, too. "Why didn't you make it sweeter?" her father continues, but Mother says nothing, just pulls on her cigarette, finishes her wine.

Delaney leaves her mother and father to stare at each other, their silence follows her down the hall like smoke. Funny how her parents never talk about the stillness that surrounds like sticky black tar. She goes to bed hungry for something she can't define, something that cannot be chewed. It's a disheveled night, hollowed out from the inside, a night of birds flapping too close to the house, of shadows with scales, forked tongues and detachable silver tails. The kind of night for wearing machine gun shoes.

Delaney wakes up the next morning to the unusual presence of Grandma Kaye. Her face is somber and she says that mother got sick during the night and went to the hospital. Everyone hopes she can come home soon, but first she has to get electric shark treatments. She asks her Grandmother what kind of disease would require such drastic measures. All Grandmother will say is that mother took bad medicine from the drawer. She was drinking too.

Alcohol, Seconal, Phenobarbital. Delaney thinks it makes a good rhyme, such nice words to be so dangerous. Alcohol, Seconal, Phenobarbital. "Nothing to worry about," says Grandma Kaye with a bright, frozen smile.

❑

When mother finally comes home sometime later, she looks mauled. Even though her father explains what happened at the hospital, Delaney thinks she is right about those sharks.

She is at the table when Mother enters and looks around as though she has not been here before. Her daughter, eating a bowl of cherries from the back yard, doesn't look up.

Mother looks at the room as though she has never inhaled its left-over fat smells, stood on its marbleized linoleum squares or watched the clock that runs too fast. She sighs and shrugs her shoulders as though the kitchen is a too large dress that she is trying on for size. The only thing she does is ask if the cat has been fed, and then she gives the animal a big, friendly hug. Mostly she looks straight ahead, out the window to the cherry tree.

Grandma makes dinner and chatters on. Walter Winchell says the war news is promising, perhaps Truman is a good president after all, although he certainly is a yokel. Everyone acts as though mother has simply been away on vacation.

Mother's eyes aren't dead anymore, but the light in them has been bent and they have taken on a peculiar cast, as though something dark is seeping in. Delaney looks at Mother and sees that where there had once been vacancy, now there is void, where once there were Broadway songs, now Mother has a tuneless, circular whistle. She smokes more often than before, leaves one cigarette burning while she lights another. She looks at the family as though they have been rented for the occasion and eats as though under water.

Delaney helps Grandma clean up. Grandma clucks as she Brillos the pots until they shine with fatigue, purges every crumb from the counters and tables, as though Mother's improvement depends on these small acts of faith. She has to take two city buses to get to her son's house and lets them all know how much she's sacrificed.

Delaney watches her mother's empty motions and wonders if she ever had a dream, wanted machine gun shoes, or wanted to fly out of the sticky silence. All she knows is that something has been peeled off her Mother, like tree bark. Something important has been taken away from this woman and what little is left, her mother will give to the cat.

❏

Phoebe Frank
© 1996

How Much is a Free Cat Worth?

AT A TIME WHEN THE WORLD KNOWS SO MUCH ABOUT HATE, I watched Tiger nursing and began to think about love. Tiger is a cat that called at my grandchildrens house, and never left. Now she's nourishing her kittens on home brew. When our own children were young, they had a cat named El Katoodles, a corruption of the Spanish, El Gato. The "oodles," like all inspiration, came unbidden. Sometimes we called her Elkness, for no reason at all. Judy, our daughter, age nine, wanted a cat and to put her off, my husband and I said, If you can find a free one advertised in the newspaper and the owner will deliver, you can get a cat. Much to our chagrin, Judy searched the want ads diligently and found a family willing to deliver a free kitten, which arrived in a cardboard carton one Sunday morning.

We had to get her shots, buy feeding and water bowls, and after she eventually became a mother, we had her spayed. Soon, we were the ones giving away free kittens, driving them to their prospective owners homes. With a feeding bowl, and a box of food as an added incentive.

Our kitty summered in Catland, an upper meow hotel for cats in Bethesda, Maryland, where we lived at the time. Catland was a two-acre haven; a woodsy site with cherry trees and dogwood abloom in the spring. When we moved from Bethesda to New Jersey, we bought her the cage to fly in and made sure she would be in a pressurized cargo hold. When we moved from New Jersey to Los Angeles, she got the royal treatment again. Through the years, the children lavished time and attention on her. We bought her the best catfood, took her in for checkups to the vet, and when she became ill in her seventeenth year, we paid the doctor bills, and worried over her health. Some free cat, I thought.

Then one day, after much fierce discussion, my husband and I decided that Elkness would have to go to that royal Catland in the sky. My hands were shaking as I put her in her big cage for the last time. We took her to the vet, where they assured us that she would not suffer. The procedure was to be done in a few hours, at five oclock. Trembling I took my leave. The children were grown and out of the house, and they didnt want to hear anything about El Katoodle's last meows. My husband and I said very little on the way home to our house in the hills of Calabasas. We live at the end of a cul-de-sac isolated from the rest of the houses in our tract. Its a beautiful area through which deer, an occasional fox, racoon, and coyotes still track. In fact, in twenty years, two bobcats had stopped in to visit. Hardly did anyones pets bother to trudge up our long driveway.

That evening around five oclock, the time we usually fed her, I heard the unmistakable sound of a cat mewing for food. It sounded so much like Elkness, that forgetting for an instant what was supposed to be happening to her at that very moment, I opened the door, fully expecting her little black self to slide in. But there was no cat. Nary a sign. Yet that disembodied Cheshire meow had materialized from somewhere; even my husband heard it. I am sure, though I cannot prove it, that the call came from that Super Deluxe Catland in the sky, that El Katoodles had paused a moment on her bright upward journey, to say good-bye.

What does a free cat cost? All the love and time and money you shower on it. All the caring you bring to the relationship is the price and the worth of a cat. And I think, maybe that's what love is; nothing glitzy. Just the simple ordinary things you do to take care of an animal or a person. That you love them and feed them, and get the best help you can when they get sick, that you help them earn their oldness. And that love is what you invest in a relationship. So that after they've gone, and they call you from that Great Place in the Sky, you'll remember how much they gave you.

❑

Writing a Story is Writing a Golem

When I wrote about little Eva Marcus creating a *golem,* I did not realize I was describing about the writing process. Writers create beings who, if they are made well, take on a life of their own. Our beings are drawn from our imagination, and when we set them down on paper, we create a world the reader can enter, and *voilla,* the entities are taken into the mind and heart of another person,

Eva's motive is different from, say Rabbi Loew's motive in creating a *golem,* all she wants is a friend, but she finds out that just like real friends, Lem (her *golem*) begins to put her own ideas into practice.

I think when we create something, be it a business, a school, a service, a piece of writing, music, or art, we never know for sure where it will take us. The product of such activity will have a mind of its own. I think that creating is one of the most Godlike activities we can share. The making of a being out of the dust of nothing, is the process God used to create Man. And I think sometimes, that He got more than he bargained for, too.

Acknowledgements

For their editorial advice and moral support not just in writing but in all ways: Charney Herst, Ph.D., my sister Phyllis Pearson, and daughters Dori Kremer and Judy Rothenberg (who laughed a lot at my elf story.) To Dan, our son, who may well have inherited the writing gene.

To Shelly Kremer whose travails with her mother in Girl Scout Cookie campaigns have inspired *Quadrant G.* To Rona and Tammy Kremer, Jessica and Rachel Rothenberg who are truly all the Jewels in my crown.

To Betty Wagner Kramer and Stefanie Simon, Administrator and Executive Director of the Wagner Human Service Training Program at the University of Judaism who have been mentors and friends along the way. And finally to all my students in the Wagner Program whose own lives are much more interesting and poignant than anything I could dream up.

Special thanks to Bob Bleiweiss, Editor and Publisher of the *Jewish Spectator,* and David Epstein, publisher of the Isaac Nathan Publishing Co., whose magazines have printed my work. To Rabbi Levi Meir for his words of wisdom and encouragement.